THE SECRET OF SUCCESS

To THE SUCCESSFUL BROTHER —
BEST THING YOU DID FOR ME
WAS INTRODUCE ME TO JANET.
NOTHING BETTER EVER HAPPENED!
THANKS & ENJOY —
LAR

THE SECRET OF SUCCESS

P. Larry Rogers

To ALISON —

YOU ARE THE PERSONIFICATION
OF EVERYTHING IN THIS BOOK.
READ AND YOU'LL UNDERSTAND,
ENJOY —
LAR

ISBN: 979-8-218-29333-8

**Ten percent of the proceeds from the sale of this book will go to the
Vascular Birthmarks Foundation.**

Cover design by LACreative.
Page layout by Win-Win Words LLC.

Printed in the United States of America.

This book is dedicated to my first grandchild, Lila Ruth Bracey. The best way I can describe her is "more than a grandchild." Some men go through a midlife crisis; Lila has taken me through a midlife delight. Before she was born, I had chosen my perfect grandfather's name—"Daddy Rog." But when Lila heard those words as toddler, they sounded like "Daah" ... a grandfather name I dearly cherish. It is my prayer that these words from Daah will bring Lila a fraction of the joy she has brought me.

contents

Prologue:
The Discovery

How would you define success? What's the secret? Is it mostly financial? Mostly mental? When you see the word *success*, who comes to mind? Who was the most successful person of your childhood? Why?

He became a millionaire at age eighteen after inheriting his dad's oil business and eventually became the richest man in the world. In the 1920s, he produced the classic movies *Hell's Angels*, *Scarface*, and *The Outlaw*. In 1935 he broke the record for air speed by flying 352 miles per hour. Later that year he broke the record for a transcontinental flight, going from California to New Jersey in seven and a half hours. He would eventually become the founder of Trans World Airlines (TWA), which he sold for $500 million in 1966. His net worth swelled to $1.5 billion, and he was the richest man in the world.

But he was a reclusive, social degenerate who spent the last years of his life in virtual seclusion. He was rarely seen by anyone except a few attendants. He worked long hours alone in a dark Las Vegas hotel suite. In one of his last photos, he had a scraggly beard down to his waist and filthy hair that hadn't been trimmed in years. His fingernails were two inches long. When he died, he had no known direct descendants or immediate family, and he didn't leave an official last will and testament. Did Howard Hughes discover the secret of success?

He was the first person on his father's side of the family to graduate high school, but he eventually rose from peanut farmer to president of the United States. He was in office only one term as his presidency was marred by an energy crisis, Soviet aggression, and the Iranian hostage crisis. When he became president, he put the peanut business in a blind trust to avoid a conflict of interest, but when he left the White House in 1981, he learned the business was $1 million in debt.

He was forced to sell and began authoring books to generate income. He has written more than thirty manuscripts. One of his most noble accomplishments is teaching a Sunday school class at Maranatha Baptist in Plains, Georgia for forty years. At this writing, he is still teaching every Sunday at age ninety-seven. In 2002 he was awarded the Nobel Peace Prize for his untiring efforts to find peaceful solutions for international conflicts. He has been involved in building 157 houses with Habitat for Humanity. Is Jimmy Carter the definition of success?

She was born in Macedonia to a financially comfortable Albanian family. By age twelve Agnes Bojaxhiu knew she wanted to dedicate her life to Christ. She left home at age eighteen for Loreto Abbey, a convent in Dublin, Ireland, never again to see her parents or sisters. In 1931, after being transferred to a convent in Mentally, India, she changed her name to Teresa to honor Saints Therese of Lisieux and Teresa of Avila. She taught high school history and geography in Calcutta for fifteen years but was distressed by poverty. In 1946, after attending a retreat in Darjeeling, she realized her true calling was among the poorest of the poor.

She left a life of comparative comfort to start a difficult life of begging. With no equipment or supplies, she began instructing poor children in Calcutta to read and write by scratching words in dirt with a stick. She was awarded the Nobel Peace Prize in 1971 but refused to attend the banquet, requesting instead that the $192,000 budget be given to help the poor of India. She died in 1997 at age eighty-seven and was later canonized in St. Peter's Square. Was Mother Teresa the standard for success?

He was born in Austria in 1947 and became Mr. Universe by age twenty. He once spent seven days in an Austrian jail for skipping rank to compete in the Junior Mr. Europe bodybuilding contest, which he won! He would eventually be named Mr. Olympia six years in a row and author several books about healthy living including *The New Encyclopedia of Modern Bodybuilding*. His childhood dream was to star in a movie, which came true with *Conan the Barbarian*, *The Terminator*, *Predator*, and many others.

He married into the political Kennedy family through his wife Maria and would be elected two-term California governor. He started the broadest sweeping health-care reform in state history, initiating physical fitness standards for schools. He was appointed by President George H. W. Bush to be chair of the President's Council on Physical Fitness. His net worth at age seventy-five is $450 million. Is Arnold Schwarzenegger the specimen of success?

He was one of the most popular people who ever walked on the Earth. When he died, 80,000 people viewed his body to pay respects. More than 200 million bought at least one of his records. When he appeared on *The Ed Sullivan Show* in 1956, 80 percent of the viewing audience tuned in. He performed 1,684 concerts in his lifetime and earned $100 million per year during the 1960s!

But his life was one tragic event after another. He adored his mother who died at age forty-six of acute liver disease. His wife divorced him after only five years of marriage, and his business manager, Colonel Tom Parker, swindled much of his money. He died due to heart failure at age forty-two after years of drug abuse. At his death he had only $5 million in the bank and was in deep debt. Did Elvis Presley find the secret of success?

The presidency, money, health, faith, friends, fame . . . which most defines success? Which of those people discovered the secret? Who lived the happiest life? Herman Cain, American businessman and one-time presidential candidate, once said, "Success is the key to happiness, and happiness is the key to success." We all want to be successful because we all want to be happy. It never goes out of style. I've never gotten out of bed one single morning and thought, *I sure hope I can be unhappy today.* No, I'm trying to be happy and fulfilled every day. And I've learned success is an inside job—feeling good about myself from the inside out. But what's the inside secret?

I was born into this world with a birthmark on my face also known as a congenital nevus. A dark skin area discolored the left side of my face, including my left eye. In 1957 plastic surgery was performed on me in infancy, and the surgeon recommended that skin be grafted from my stomach to cover the nevus. A sliver of skin was taken from my lower abdomen and grafted to the left side of my face. The new skin was successfully attached and covered most of the brown nevus. Another surgeon performed additional surgery in my late thirties, removing the skin graft and reconfiguring the area with a tissue expander.

I've learned success is not outer but inner. Marilyn Monroe had one of the most beautiful outers but was miserable inside. The same was true for Naomi Judd. Success and fame are not synonymous. I once heard a man speak who has no arms or legs, but he had the attitude of a champion. I knew another who damaged his spinal cord in a diving accident and spent his life in a wheelchair. He had a positive outlook, became an elected county official, and gave away 250 acres that became a church camp. I knew another man who was a dwarf. His height was four feet, but his sense of humor was the tallest in his class. He graduated college, became a CPA, and eventually mayor of his town. *I can* is more important than *IQ*.

The inspiration for my life is my grandfather, J. Glendon Johns. He was a farmer who had all odds stacked against him. His dad parceled out the large family farm; since Glendon was the youngest, he received the least and poorest allotment. Then on D-Day (June 6, 1944), as Army Rangers were scaling the cliffs at Pont-du-Hoc, he was unclogging a crop reaper and got his hand caught in the machine. He not only lost his hand but most of his arm. It looked like a gangrene infection would cost him his life. He was the first person in Rutherford County (Tennessee) to be administered penicillin. It was a brave last-ditch effort that saved his life.

And then a few years after the accident, "Dadyn" received word his farm would be taken by the government as part of forming Percy Priest Lake. He was forced to move. He moved from Rutherford to Wilson County and started again, farming 600 acres with 300 cows and one arm. It was his right arm, and he was left-handed. But when he died in 1991 at age eighty, he left behind an estate of over $1 million while most 'two-armed' farmers in his community were barely making ends meet.

I don't know if it was because I was his firstborn grandchild or because we both loved the great outdoors, but we enjoyed a special relationship. He was best man in my wedding and best influence in my life. He was a man's man who never complained or blamed. If he could find the right success with his wrong arm, you can, too.

So, if success is defined by inner peace and outer joy, then exactly how is it achieved? What's the secret? Is it mostly physical? Mostly social? Financial? Spiritual?

Success Is a Whole Number

Aristotle was the first to coin the phrase "The whole is greater than the sum of its parts." An auto parts store is stocked with parts that are worthless unless they are installed to run a whole vehicle. The visceral organs in the body are only functional if they interact with each other in the whole body. And I enjoy squash casserole, but only if the ingredients are perfectly mixed to create a whole casserole.

Real peace and happiness are found when the *whole* person is developed for physical, social, financial, and spiritual success. You develop *all* those qualities to achieve real success. Your whole life is filled with mental peace and genuine happiness when your whole person becomes greater than the sum of its parts. *That's the secret!*

Real success is not an accomplishment in one area but proficiency in all four. Our education system is designed to provide instruction for the whole curriculum of life. If you're good at math but can't speak using proper grammar, your success will be soiled. An entertainer may sell 200 million records and have 200 million friends but be broke and alone with drug and spending addictions. The ordinary person focuses on the parts of life they're trying to receive while the successful person focuses on the whole life they're trying to accomplish.

William Howard Taft was so overweight he got stuck in a bathtub. He was president of the United States but at four hundred pounds could hardly walk. He spent his last few years in a wheelchair and died at age seventy-two with heart disease and high blood pressure. President Thomas Jefferson built Monticello, one of the most cherished homes in America, but he was in deep debt. He died in 1826, leaving arrears of $107,000, equivalent to $3 million today. Vince Young, quarterback of the Tennessee Titans, was in perfect physical shape and received a $26 million rookie contract but spent it faster than he could cash it. Seven years after receiving that wad, he filed for Chapter 11 bankruptcy. Steve Jobs founded Apple in 1976 and is largely responsible for the explosion of tech in our lives. But he was a self-proclaimed Buddhist who began wondering about the existence of God in his last few days. He was asked if he was a believer and responded, "Yes, but not in the ordinary sense. I believe there's something . . . some presence. Consciousness. It's like a wheel." He lived with a void that could never be filled by Wi-Fi or web browsers. Real success is not measured by achievement in one aspect of life but by developing the whole person physically, socially, financially, and spiritually.

It's always a sad day when a long life ends without real accomplishment. No financial security, no friends, no proactive health, and no spiritual contentment. If success is one of the best words, failure is one of the worst. You don't want your memoirs to start with the word *Unfortunately*.

What is your peace and joy barometer reading today? Do others see you as happy and successful? On a scale of 1-10, how would you rate your satisfaction with life?

Success Is Never Too Late

One day I was working as a pastor in Kennett, Missouri, when my church secretary received a call in the office from the local hospital. The caller said, "We have a patient who just threatened a nurse with a knife. Now he wants to meet with a pastor. Would yours be willing?" I agreed to go.

As I slowly cracked open his door, I quickly saw a defeated man. He was covered in bad tattoos before they were cool, and he was sobbing. I asked him to tell me his situation, and he said with tears, "I'm dying and going to hell, and there's nothing anybody can do about it." He had spent most of his life in prison for killing two people. He was divorced and estranged from his children. He was not only dying but dying alone and broke. No friends, no accomplishments, no money, and no hope in the next life.

I asked if he'd ever been a churchgoer. He said his grandmother took him a few times when he was a boy. I continued, "Did anybody in Sunday School teach you about the apostle Paul or King David? Do you realize that they did things worse than you, and still found favor with God." I continued, "King David took another man's wife and had her husband killed. He became a man after God's own heart! The apostle Paul persecuted and murdered Christians but ended up writing most of the New Testament. Have you done anything as bad as those guys?"

I'll never forget his response. He got up out of bed and pulled out his IV needle. With blood trickling down his arm he asked, "Will you take my confession and baptize me?" We walked arm-in-arm out the door of his room, down the hall to the elevator. The nurses turned pale as we passed their station! We went downstairs to the whirlpool tub. I baptized him and as he came up out of the water soaking wet, he bear-hugged me. It was the best moment of his broken life. I preached at his funeral a few weeks later which was the second-best day of his life. It's never too late to start over; never too late to get started; never too late to avoid the *Unfortunately.*

Success is not a destination, but an exciting adventure. I've noticed America's wealthiest people experience joy on the journey. That's one of the most appealing aspects. Sailing is as pleasurable as reaching the harbor. Alexander the Great wept because there were no more worlds to conquer. It wasn't the conquered but the conquering that rushed the adrenalin. The thrill of shopping for a new car is nearly as thrilling as owning. Life is not a race to the finish but an embrace of one precious day at a time.

The thrill of making a new friend, losing fifty pounds, saving that first $50,000, or finding peace deep down in the soul are 'joy on the journey' experiences. There is no station in life to which we arrive for the last time. It's an unending adventure and the efficacious learn to relish each new morning.

Pass It On

The Jewish race has been regarded by some as having the highest level of intelligence. Some have theorized that since Jews were God's chosen people, they have a higher IQ than other ethnic groups. A *New York Times* writer got in trouble for writing that Jews are only 3 percent of the population but have won 27 percent of the U.S. Nobel science prizes. But the most impressive thing about them is their willingness to pass along information to the next generation.

Neuroscientists believe the human brain can hold up to 100 terabytes (100,000 GB) of data. That's more information than is on the entire worldwide web! It gives me a headache to type those words. My laptop has a mere 128 GBs of RAM or memory. When a wise person dies, all that knowledge and wisdom are gone. Moses told the Israelites to "repeat his words again and again to the children and grandchildren." He reminded them, "Talk about them when you sit at home and when you walk along the road, when you lie down and when you get up." In other words, pass along the terabytes to the next generation. Recording artist Sandi Patty was asked to define success and said, "As an artist, it would be perhaps that I've learned enough in my journey that I would have something worthwhile to pass on to the next generation." Knowledge is power, but knowledge shared is power multiplied.

This book is the first in a series intended to pass along my life's learning to my grandchildren . . . and all God's children. This is not a children's book or religious book or family book, but one about finding the true secret of success for *all*.

I've walked on this Earth twenty-five thousand days and moved to a new address eleven times. I'm a parent and a grandparent. I grew up in a small town but spent most of my life in a big city. I've owned a landscape design business, been an ordained pastor for three denominations, and a licensed health insurance agent. I've never stopped learning because life has never stopped teaching.

I have enjoyed reading self-help books and always dreamed of writing one. I've been mentally processing this book for fifteen years. I've read books by Dale Carnegie, Norman Vincent Peale, Joel Osteen, Stephen Covey, Zig Ziglar, Viktor Frankl, Napoleon Hill, Louise L. Hay, and Rick Warren. I've enjoyed the autobiographies of great men such as Sam Walton, Ronald Reagan, Billy Graham, Bill Gates, Steve Jobs, and Winston Churchill. One of my newest interests is cooking, and I'm an avid student of Mediterranean diet cookbooks. I'm the chief chef at our house. I'm a daily Bible reader and have read it completely twenty-five times. And perhaps my favorite topic is investing. I've been investing in the stock market almost every day for forty years. I've read the writings of Warren Buffett, Peter Lynch, John Bogle, Ben Graham, Andrew Aziz, Dave Ramsey, and William Bernstein. We are most powerful when we share knowledge instead of hoard it. When we learn, we teach; when we teach, we learn.

A benchmark is a gauge or standard by which others are measured. A chef's original recipe is the standard or benchmark for other cooks to emulate. The Dow Jones, S&P, and Nasdaq are benchmark stock indexes by which others are compared. The word *benchmark* originates from a chiseled indention in a concrete slab into which the feet of a bench leg are placed. Benchmarks ensure the bench can be repositioned into the same level place each time. The benchmarks of success are four marks or standards that position and reposition your life, keeping it level, balanced, and successful.

I chose the book's title because everybody wants in on a secret, and because everybody wants in on a successful life. Let's be in on it together. Keep your eyes open for the tongue-in-cheekers and a few bad jokes. Smiling is the universal language.

"The problem with quotes on the Internet is you can never be sure they're authentic."
—**Abraham Lincoln**

THE SECRET OF SUCCESS

1

THE PHYSICAL

THE FIRST BENCHMARK IS PHYSICAL HEALTH. It is impossible to be very happy if you're very hurting. You might have a good attitude and march through every day with a smile on your face, but pain is no fun. No pain, no gain might sound exciting on the football field but not in everyday life. If the health benchmark is not properly chiseled into the success platform, your life will be wobbly. Health is the best hobby.

Although sickness and pain are ultimately inevitable, a successful life tries to postpone them with diet and exercise. The worst hobbies are doctor visits and prescription pills. Having worked in health insurance and ministry, I've been with some who seemed to think health issues are the best hobby. They knew the details of every pill. The victim mentality was their ticket.

When I was growing up in smalltown Centerville, Tennessee, in the late sixties, our local dentist started jogging on the city streets. Most everybody thought he'd lost his mind. I remember cars slowing down and staring at him as though he needed to jog on over to the mental health clinic. He was ruining his legs, for heaven's sake! Why would he do that to himself?

Other rumors suggested he'd given up sugar and was eating mostly whole grains, fruits, and vegetables. What?? Trading granny's chocolate meringue pie for granola? I remember seeing a loaf of Roman Meal bread on his kitchen table. He must have lost his mind. Romans don't know anything about tasty bread! As it turned out, many who were critical of Dr. Blackwell the house . . . and they were delicious. I've read that ten thousand brain cells die every day, but those stinkin' fat cells have eternal life!

Desserts Spelled Backward Is *Stressed*

The extraction of sugar from the sugar cane bush originated in India four thousand years ago. The word *sugar* comes from the Hindu word *sakkara* meaning ground or candied sugar. As Christopher Columbus was about to leave Spain, he loaded sugar cane plants onto the *Nina*, *Pinta*, and *Santa Maria* and planted them in the Caribbean because of suitable climate. The top sugarcane plantations are in Guyana, Jamaica, Belize, and Barbados, producing 90 percent of sugar consumed in Western Europe. We've had a fatal attraction to *sakkara* for a long, sweet time. Bubba said, "If we are what we eat, I should be the sweetest guy in town!"

Growing up in the South with pecan pie, banana pudding, chocolate cake, butter cookies, and just a spoonful of sugar in everything, nothing so delights my taste buds. A meal was not finished until dessert was served . . . with a dollop of Cool Whip on top. Research shows that children have an affection for confection at an early age. If given the choice, babies will select a sweeter formula. The problem is not that we have a sweet tooth, we have a mouth full of them! And yes, I'm the guy who likes a little pumpkin pie with my Cool Whip.

But with modern research, we know a lot about the negative side effects of sugar. It's a major player in heart disease and bad cholesterol (LDL). It might be linked to Alzheimer's disease and causes glucose levels to spike and plummet. It accelerates aging, causes tooth decay and acne, disables appetite control, and is addictive. The American Heart Association suggests women consume no more than six teaspoons of sugar per day, nine for men. One twelve-ounce soda has 9.75 grams!

One of the worst encounters with sugar is carbonated beverages. They're on the Who's Who list of fatal foods. Weight gain, tooth decay, insulin resistance, metabolic syndrome, dehydration, bloating, and stomach lining damage are all waiting in a shiny can. A friend once told me about leaving a pencil in a glass of soda overnight and waking up to find the yellow paint eroded from the wood. The ingredients in a twelve-ounce can of Coke include high fructose corn syrup, the carcinogenic chemical 4-MEI, phosphoric acid, aspartame, caffeine, and 140 calories.

But yes, I know a can of Coke is the real thing for millions worldwide! It has been one of the best performing stocks of all-time and at this writing

Warren Buffett owns 400 million shares. If you're young and haven't started, don't. And although no one likes a quitter, you'll be forgiven for curtailing carbonation.

"Everything in moderation" are three good words for one healthy life. The good Lord created food, money, sex, work, rest, exercise, pets, hobbies, vacations, Wi-Fi, and wine. They're all good, but better and best when enjoyed in moderation. A successful life is having some of everything but not an excess of anything. Both carrots and cookies are fine, if moderate. A diet of all carrots or all cookies is not salubrious.

Work and personal life are two sides of the same coin, supporting and reciprocating each other. Neither workaholic nor playboy is a healthy lifestyle. Addiction is the opposite of moderation. I remember my dad telling me early in life that the older we get, the tougher it is to break an addiction. Make an early commitment to moderation and you'll be habit free later.

Two Weeks of Dieting . . . Lost 14 days

The four most important benefits of a healthy diet are:

- Improving cholesterol levels
- Reducing blood pressure
- Managing body weight
- Controlling blood sugar

There are numerous diet plans including Atkins, Keto, Vegan, Weight Watchers, and South Beach, but nothing works better than combining exercise with calorie counting. Whether it's the bank account or calorie count, exact knowledge is crucial. The number on the scales starts going down when calorie awareness starts going up. I use a Samsung health app to tally the callies and digital kitchen scales for weighing foods. The best unit of measurement is grams. Food is fuel, not therapy.

The key to reducing weight is not exercise but discipline in the pantry. Abs are made in the kitchen. Exercise helps the body use calories more efficiently but doesn't burn many fat cells. One hour of vigorous training burns the number of calories in a handful of peanuts. Food knowledge and calorie counting are crucial. A bowl of oatmeal has only 154 calories, a cup of Greek yogurt 150, a large egg 72, a piece of baked fish 60, and a cup of cottage cheese 163. Those are manageable numbers and fill the tummy just like a tater tot.

At one point my weight was 185 pounds and I wanted 165. I counted the calories of every bite and realized 2,500 per day would maintain my current weight. My callies needed a cut. I reduced them to 2,000 and began seeing results. A step-up on the bathroom scales was a step down on the insurance weight chart. I keep my weight at around 160-165 pounds with 1,500-1,800 daily calories. I also work out three or four days per week. The formula is different for everybody, but it's all mind over *fatter*. Health is the best hobby.

On the following page (page 7) is the chart I use to record food and weight. This is based on a diet of 1,500-1,800 daily calories. Your numbers will vary depending on the calorie total.

A healthy diet is not just focused on calories but also considers the percentages of carbohydrate, fat, and protein—approximately 45% carbs, 30% fats, and 25% protein. Percentages vary depending on activity. When you input a food into the online health app, it displays carbs/fat/protein percentages, along with other nutrients.

Huge strides have been made in medical research in the last fifty years with one of the most beneficial being nutrition. We now understand the chemistry of foods and exactly how the body processes them. A major advancement is the *glycemic index*—a numeric value that measures how much foods spike blood sugar and insulin levels. Foodstuffs are rated on a scale of 1-100 with a small number indicating less spike. Low GI foods include fruits, vegetables, black beans, lentils, and whole grains. They're easier for the body to digest which leads to balanced blood sugar levels. High GI foods include potato chips, soda, sweet tea, cheeseburger, donuts, and French fries. Just as you surmised! They spike blood sugar levels, which increases the risk of type 2 diabetes, heart disease, and some cancers. There are websites that give the glycemic index or *load* for foods including glycemicindex.com.

A few years ago, I made a spreadsheet with a list of my top 100 foods which included their numeric value for calories, omega-3 & omega-6 fatty acids, protein, fiber, glycemic load, total fat, potassium, carbs, vitamin K, magnesium, sodium and vitamin B-12. Health is the best hobby. You can see a version of my spreadsheet scaled down to fit on the five pages beginning on page 9.

Day	Mon	Tues	Wed	Thurs	Fri	Sat	Sun	Avg
Weight								
Calories (1500-1800)								
Carbs 40-50%								
Fats 35-40%								
Protein 15-20%								
Protein (80-120g)								
Fiber (30g)								
Potassium (3500 mg)								
Vitamin A (900 µg)								
Vitamin C (90mg)								
Calcium (750-1000mg)								
Iron (8 mg /day)								
Saturated Fat 10g								
Sodium (<1300 mg)								
Water (48 ozs)								
Min. aerob exer. (7 hrs/wk)								
Breakfast calories								
Lunch calories								
Dinner calories								

It's All Greek to Me

The April 2017 edition of *National Geographic* magazine included a study of the lifestyle and environment of the healthiest people in the world based on the percentage of their community who lived more than one hundred years. The centenarians were said to live in blue zones because author Dan Buettner circled their locations on a map with a blue ink pen. Those included Okinawa, Japan; Sardinia, Italy; Nicoya, Costa Rica; Ikaria, Greece; and, Loma Linda, California. They all shared nine lifestyle habits called the Power 9:

- Active each day with physical activity (gardening, walking to the market, etc.).
- Wake up each morning with a sense of purpose.
- Downshift through prayer or a nap when stress is overwhelming.
- Stop eating during a meal when still hungry (80% stomach full rule).
- Eat beans as their primary food.
- Drink one to two glasses of red wine per day.
- Regularly attend church or other faith-based community.
- Enjoy a long marriage and/or put family first.
- Cultivate a social life with friends.

Blue zone residents ate the Mediterranean diet. *U.S. News & World Report* ranked it No. 1 on their list of the forty best diets for 2022, citing a "host of health benefits, including weight loss, heart and brain health, cancer prevention, and diabetes control." Great credentials!

A Med diet breakfast might include a combination from the following list. Keep the calorie count to 500-700 when breaking the fast:

- Boiled egg
- Canned meats in water (tuna, chicken, fish)
- Beans/peas
- Steel-cut oatmeal
- Baked chicken
- Baked pork chop
- Avocado
- Homemade whole grain bread

FOOD	CALS	PROTEIN	FIBER	FOOD	TOTAL FAT	POTASH	CARBS
*Almonds (1 oz, 23 nuts)	162	6.0g	3.4g	0	14.0g	199mg	6.1g
Almond butter (100g)	98			0			
*Anchovies (5 fish)	42	5.8g	0	0	1.9g	109mg	0
Apple (1 medium)	94	0.5g	4.4g	5	0.3g	195mg	25.1g
Artichoke (Jeru, raw, 100g)	73	2g	1.6g	7	0	429mg	17.4g
Arugula (raw, 100g)	25			2			
Asparagus (100g)	20	2.2g	2.1g	2	0	202mg	4g
*Avocado (raw, 1 fruit, 201g)	322	4g	13.5g	4	29.5g	975mg	17g
Avocado oil (1 tbsp)	124	0	0	0	14g	0	0
Banana (1 medium)	105	1.3g	3.1g	10	0.5g	422mg	27g
Beans (black, cooked, 100g)	111	7.5g	7.5g	8	0.45g	305mg	20.4g
Beans (green, 100g cooked)	34.1	2.0g	3.7g	3	0.1g	230mg	7.8g
Beans (pinto, 100g cooked)	120	7.5g	7.5g	9	1.1g	360mg	22.4g
Beets (100g, raw)	22	2.2g	3.7g	1			
Blueberries (100g)	57	0.7g	2.4g	4	0.3g	77mg	14.5g
Broccoli (spears, 100g)	29	3.1g	3.0g	2	0.3g	250mg	5.3g
Brussel Spr (cook, 1/2c, 78g)	28	2.0g	2.0g	2	0.4g	247mg	5.5g
Cabbage (1 cup)	22	1.1g	2.2g	2			
Cantaloupe (1 wedge, 69g)	23.5	0.6g	0.6g	2	0.1g	184mg	6.1g
Carrot (1 med, 61g)	25	0.6g	1.7g	2	0.1g	195mg	5.8g
Cayenne pepper (1 tsp)	5.6	0.2g	0.5g	0			
Celery (1 med stalk)	6.4	0.3g	0.6g	0	0.1g	104mg	1.4g
Chard (100g, cooked)	20	1.9g	2.1g	2			
Cherries (100g)	46	0.9g	1.6g	5	0.4g	124mg	11g
*Chia seeds (1 oz, 28g)	137	4.4g	10.6g	1			

FOOD	CALS	PROTEIN	FIBER	FOOD	TOTAL FAT	POTASH	CARBS
Chickpeas (cooked, 100g)	135	7.2g	6	10	4.2g	235mg	22.5g
Chicken (breast, 100g)	110	23.1g	0	0	1.2g	255mg	0
Cinnamon (1 tsp, 2g)	6.2	0.1g	1.3g	0			
Clams (1 can, 5.5 oz)	79.7	1.0g	0.7g	6	0.3g	148mg	18.2g
*Coconut Oil (1 tbsp)	119	0	0	0			0
Cod (Atlantic, 1 filet, 239g)	189	41.1g	0	0	1.5g	954mg	0
Coffee (1 c)	0			0			
Coriander (1 tsp)	5.2	0.2g	0.7g	0			
Corn (cooked, 100g)	88	3g	2.4g	10	0.8g	210mg	20g
Cranberry juice (1/2 c, unsw)	58	.5g	0.15g	4	0.15g	95mg	15g
Couscous (100g, cooked)	80	3g	1.1g	12	13.5g		
Curry (1 tbsp)	20	0.8g	2.1g	1	0.9g	96.4mg	3.6g
*Dark chocolate (1 oz, 28g)	168	2.2g	3.1g	15	12g	200mg	12.8g
Edamame (100g)	110	10.3g	4.8g	4	4.7g	482mg	9.8g
*Egg (large, boiled)	77	6.3g	0	1	5.3g	63mg	0.6g
Eggplant (raw, 100g)	24	1g	3.4g	1	0.2g	230mg	5.7g
Farro (1 oz)	89	2.8g	1.7g	10			17.9g
Fennel (bulb, raw)	27	1.1g	2.7g	2	0.2g	360mg	6.3g
*Flax seed (1 tbsp, whole)	54	1.9g	2.8g	0			
Garlic (3 cloves)	13.4	0.6g	0.2	1	0	36.1mg	3g
Grapefruit (1/2 fruit, 123g)	51	0.9g	2g	4	0.2g	166mg	13.1g
Great Grains (2/3 cup)	210	4g	5g	24			
Green beans (100g, raw)	31			3			
Green peas (100g, cooked)	134	8.6g	8.8g	6	0.4g	434mg	25g
*Hazelnuts (10 nuts, 14g)	87.9	2.1g	1.4g	0	8.5g	95.2mg	2.3g

FOOD	CALS	PROTEIN	FIBER	FOOD	TOTAL FAT	POTASH	CARBS
*Herring (1 filet, raw)	291	33g	0	0	16g	602mg	
Honey (1 tbsp)	63	0.1g	0	10	0	10.9mg	17.3g
Lentils (cooked, 100g)	363	25.8g	30.5g	10	1.1g	955mg	60g
Kale (100g)	10.1	0.9g	0.6g	1	0.2g	125mg	2.8g
Kashi 7-whole grain (1/2c)	180	12g	13.0g	27	2g	390mg	40g
Kiwi (raw, 100g)	61	1.1g	1.1g	4	0.5g	312mg	14.7g
Lima beans (cooked, 1c)	209			15			
*Macadamia nuts (10-12)	203	2.2g	2.4g	0	21.4g	104mg	4g
*Mackerel (cooked, 3 oz)	223	20.3	0	0	15.1	341mg	0
Metamucil (2 tsp)	40	0	6.0g	0	0	60mg	10mg
Milk (Almond, 1 cup, unswe)	16	0.4g	0.4g	0	2.5g	72.9mg	0.8g
Mint (2 tbsp)	2.1	0.1g	0.2g	0			
Mushroom (porta, raw 100g)	26	2.5g	1.5g	3	0.2g	484mg	5.1g
Oats (Steel-cut, 1/4 cup, raw)	170	7g	5.0g	15	3g	0	29g
Okra (raw, 100g)	31	2.0g	3.2g	3	0.1g	303mg	7g
*Olive (1 oz, 28g)	32	0.2g	0.9g	0			
*Olive oil (1 tbsp)	119	0	0	0	13.5g	0.1mg	0
Onion (medium, raw)	44	1.2g	1.9g	4	0.1g	161mg	10.3g
Orange	65	1.0g	3.4g	4	0.3g	233mg	16.3g
Peaches (1 medium, 150g)	58	1.4g	2.2g	5	0.4g	285mg	14.8g
Pear (small)	85.8	0.6g	4.6g	5	1.5g	176mg	22.9g
*Peanut butter (2 tbsp)	188	8g	1.9g	0		208mg	
*Pecans (1 oz, 28g)	193	2.6g	2.7g	0	20.2g	115mg	3.9g
Pepper (green)	32	1.4g	2.8g	2	0.3g	287mg	7.6g
*Pistachio (1 oz, 49 kernels)	157	5.8g	2.9g	1	12.6g	290mg	7.9g

FOOD	CALS	PROTEIN	FIBER	FOOD	TOTAL FAT	POTASH	CARBS
Pomegranate juice (1 cup)	134	0.4g	0.2g	8	0.7g	533mg	32.7g
Pork (raw, 100g)	109	20.2g	0	0	3.1g	519mg	0
Potato (red, 100g, cooked)	123	3g	2.5g	9			
*Pumpkin seeds (1 oz, 28g)	146	9g	1.1g	0			
Quinoa (100g, cooked)	103	4.0g	2g	10	1.7g	158mg	18g
Raspberries (1oz, 28g)	28	0.2g	1.2g	2	0	31.9mg	7.3g
Rice (wild, cooked) 100g	100	4.1g	1.7g	10	0.3g	120mg	21g
*Salmon (wild) 100g/ 3.5oz	182	25.4g	0	0	8.1g	628mg	0
*Sardines (2 fish)	49	5.9g	0	0	2.7g	95.3mg	0
Sauerkraut (100g)	19			1			
Scallops (raw, 1 oz, 85g)	24	4.7g	0	1	0.2g	90mg	0.7g
Shrimp (3 oz, 85g)	84.1	17.8g	0	0	0.9g	155mg	0
Squash (summer, medium)	31	2.4g	2.2g	3	0.4g	514mg	6.6g
Split pea (raw, 1 oz, 28g)	95	6.9g	7g	6	0.3g	275mg	17g
Spinach (frozen, 100g)	34	4.0g	3.7g	1	0.9g	302mg	4.8g
Strawberry (100g, raw)	32			2			
Sweet potato (cooked- 1 med)	103	2.3g	3.8g	10	0.2g	541mg	23.6g
Tahini (1 tbsp)	85	2.7g	1.4g	0			
Tempeh (100g, cooked)	193			5			
Tofu	76			2			
Tomato (1 medium)	22	1.1g	1.5g	2	0.2g	292mg	4.8g
Tomato juice (low sod., 1 c)	53	1.5g	1.9g	3	0	467mg	11.1g
Turkey (1 oz, 28g)	44	6.1g	0	1	2g	77mg	0
*Walnut (1 oz, 28g)	173	6.7g	1.9g	0			
Watermelon (raw, 100g)	30	0.6g	0.4g	2	0.2	112mg	7.5g

FOOD	CALS	PROTEIN	FIBER	FOOD	TOTAL FAT	POTASH	CARBS
Whey protein powder (1 cup)	120	1.6g	1.5g	9	1g	193mg	26.1g
Whole wheat bread (1 slice)	128	3.9g	2.8g	5	2.5g	145mg	23.7g
Yogurt (1 cup)	233	10.8g	0	24	0.5g	475mg	46.5g
Zucchini (1 med, 196g)	31.4	2.4g	2.2g	3	0.1g	514mg	6.6g

*Smart Fats

*Most of the data in the graph came from www.nutritiondata.self.com and www.tools.myfooddata.com.

- Peaches
- Orange juice
- Olives
- Yogurt w/granola & berries
- Protein shake
- Nuts
- Tomato juice
- Grape juice
- Sweet potato
- Strawberry
- Raisins
- Quinoa
- Fried corn (fresh or frozen)
- Pomegranate juice
- Cranberry juice
- Pineapple juice
- Whole grain cereal
- Honey
- Apple (cooked and raw)
- Healthy muffins
- Prunes
- Healthy pancakes
- Whole wheat bread

- Avocado w/low-fat cottage cheese
- Pear
- Papaya
- Apricot
- Blueberries
- Baked oatmeal
- Breakfast burrito
- Breakfast wrap
- Rice
- Kale

For lunch, sample menu items include:

- Baked salmon
- Steamed asparagus
- Baked sweet potato
- Brown rice
- Quinoa
- Couscous
- Green peas
- Baked whole chicken
- Baked lean pork chop
- Avocado
- Corn on the cob
- Arugula salad
- Steamed carrots
- Homemade whole wheat bread

The calorie count should be 800-1000 for the midday dejeuner. I have several Mediterranean diet cookbooks including *The Complete Mediterranean Cookbook*, *The 30-Minute Mediterranean Diet Cookbook*, and *Mediterranean Paleo Cooking*. The recipes are tasty, easy to prepare, and make you feel like you're lunching in Santorini.

My grandparents were farmers with a diet consisting of mostly summer garden vegetables and lean meats. They were pros at canning and freezing.

They didn't call it a Mediterranean diet, but it resembled one in many ways. They were active on the farm and could check off the Power 9 lifestyle habits. Yes, my grandmother cooked with Crisco, sugar, and all things Southern, but they enjoyed good health into their eighties. Working hard on the farm has a way of forgiving a few bad bites.

When Janet and I began the Mediterranean diet, we also committed to eating only two major meals a day. The ancient Romans ate only one big meal a day! We eat a large mid-morning lunch (10 A.M.) after our morning exercise and then a smaller mid-afternoon meal/snack (3 P.M.). This meal schedule has contributed significantly to our weight control. It took a few weeks for our bodies to adjust, but they have adapted well. We also try to avoid things that make us fat like scales, mirrors, and photographs.

Mid-afternoon meal/snack suggestions:

- Mediterranean chickpea salad
- Loaded Mediterranean hummus w/ Pita chips
- Crock-Pot paleo trail mix
- Greek yogurt spinach artichoke dip
- Greek zucchini fritters
- Mediterranean nachos
- Baked phyllo chips
- Mediterranean roasted artichokes
- Kalamata olives
- Detox vegan smoothie
- Crackers and tuna salad
- Nuts and dried fruit
- Fruit slices w/nut butter
- Tomato w/feta cheese
- Pumpkin seed salsa
- Granola bars
- Baked whole grain Lavash chips w/Med dip
- Cucumber bites (cucumber w/salmon)
- Whole wheat banana blueberry muffins
- Garlic & parmesan lentil chips
- Dried organic apple

- Rice squares w/quinoa
- Falafel crunchy chickpeas
- Cucumber hummus sandwiches
- Edamame
- Cucumber bites
- Olives
- Tomato
- Tomato salsa
- Squash wedges
- Lentils stuffed potato skins

A glass of skim or 2% milk is also a good appetite suppressor. Lactose is a fast-acting carbohydrate that moves rapidly from stomach to intestines, converting carbs to blood sugar to energy.

According to nutritionists, one of the worst things for the body is late-night snacking, especially just before bedtime. Food wakes up the brain and moves the body into an active, digestive mode just before sleep. It also slows metabolism and can cause acid reflux, indigestion, and heartburn. If you eat a big meal just before sleep, you'll be counting more trips to the bathroom than sheep. If you must eat something late, choose a banana which promotes sleep because it has magnesium and potassium. Or you can eat a boiled egg which is good protein and digests quickly. Several nutrition books rank boiled egg as the No. 1 most nutritious food. If late-night junk food is a temptation, get it out of the house! 'Outta sight, outta mind' is a better diet plan than the most disciplined Atkins or South Beach.

1 Cal per Serving . . . 100 Servings per Can

It's important to read food labels. The Food and Drug Administration (FDA) monitors foods to insure they're safe, wholesome, and properly labeled. Labels include information on calories and thirteen nutrients: total fat, saturated fat, trans fat, cholesterol, sodium, carbohydrate, fiber, sugars, protein, vitamin A, vitamin C, calcium and iron, and % daily values. By law, companies must also label name, date, net weight, ingredients, nutrition information, allergy warnings, and name/address/country of food origin. Bubba said he accidentally went grocery shopping on an empty stomach and now he's the proud owner of aisle 6. Shown below is a sample of a food label listing iots nutritional composition as well as other key information.

Beware that food labels are misleading:

- *No cholesterol peanut butter.* Cholesterol is never found in plant products, only in animal products.
- *Made with whole grains* doesn't mean 100% whole grains were used—maybe just a pinch.
- *Multigrain* implies healthy but just means refined grains.
- *Natural* implies organic but means nothing.
- The label *light* doesn't meet any standard but is used only comparatively to other foods.
- *Low carb* has no guidelines.
- *Low calorie* means 120 cals or less per 100g.
- *Low fat* means just no more than 30% of the calories come from fat.
- *Grass fed* doesn't mean a cow has been eating grass its entire life but tasted it at some point.
- *Cage free* doesn't mean chickens are roaming the farm but in a barn area instead of a small cage.
- And *100% orange juice* is a head scratcher since its label lists more ingredients than just orange juice.

The best food labels are in the produce section where there are usually no labels.

Frozen vegetables are healthier than canned vegetables. Frozen means blanched (cooked in hot water, then cooled quickly). Canned means processed and contains the chemical BPA, a carcinogen. If you cook canned veggies, drain them with a strainer and rinse, then boil in fresh water and olive oil. Processed foods (canned vegetables, canned meats, soups, bread, cookies, ready-to-use meals, etc.) are tasty because they're oozing with salt, sugar, trans fat, oil, preservatives, and lots of calories. The healthiest grocery shopping is usually on the store's perimeter, not in the mid-section where the processed items are ready and weighting. Anything processed needs to be eaten less. The canned food drives won't like me!

Eat more of these foods:

- Broccoli, bananas: fiber, potassium, calcium, iron

- Milk: 2%, calcium rich
- Celery: fiber, potassium
- Orange juice w/calcium

Nutrition Facts

Serving Size 3 oz. (85g)
Serving Per Container 2

Amount Per Serving

Calories 200 Calories from Fat 120

% Daily Value*

Total Fat 15g	**20 %**
Saturated Fat 5g	**28 %**
Trans Fat 3g	
Cholesterol 30mg	**10 %**
Sodium 650mg	**28 %**
Total Carbohydrate 30g	**10 %**
Dietary Fiber 0g	**0 %**
Sugars 5g	
Protein 5g	

Vitamin A 5%	•	Vitamin C 2%	
Calcium 15%	•	Iron 5%	

*Percent Daily Values are based on a 2,000 calorie diet. Your Daily Values may be higher or lower depending on your calorie needs.

	Calories	2,000	2,500
Total Fat	Less than	65g	80g
Sat Fat	Less than	20g	25g
Cholesterol	Less than	300mg	300mg
Sodium	Less than	2,400mg	2,400mg
Total Carbonhydrate		300mg	375mg
Dietary Fiber		25g	30g

- Grapefruit: potassium, vitamin A, C
- Almonds: 5g saturated fat, fiber, protein, Vitamin E
- Whole grain cereal: fortified with vitamins/minerals
- Tuna salad: low calorie and tasty
- Carrots: vitamin A
- Salmon: omega-3 fatty acids, saturated fat, sodium, protein, vitamin A
- Mackerel: protein, omega-3 fatty acids
- Kale: vitamins C, A, K1, cancer-fighting compounds
- Garlic: lowers blood pressure, vitamins, minerals
- Shellfish: clams, oysters, shrimp, scallop, mussels
- Baked potato: very nutrient-rich food
- Beef/chicken liver: vitamins, iron, protein
- Blueberries: antioxidants, fight dementia
- Egg yolk: nutrient rich

Also on the good list are apples, romaine lettuce, tomatoes, broccoli, kale, mushrooms, beets, asparagus, lettuce, cabbage, onions, cauliflower, carrots, bell peppers, avocados, blueberries, beans, bananas, 2% milk, olives, dill pickles, Brussel sprouts, cucumbers, sweet potatoes, green beans, corn, whole grain rice, quinoa, couscous, green peas, walnuts, and turnips.

Bottom line: there are many healthy foods available without settling for fast, processed, breaded, sugared, or carbonated. Someone said, "If it's a plant, eat it; if it was made in a plant, avoid it." I never thought I'd be that guy drinking that green juice.

When googling healthy meats, beef liver tops the list. Not me! But sirloin steak pleases my taste buds. It's lean with less fat than ribeye or T-bone. I back the back! T-bone is too fatty and is two steaks attached to the same bone—strip on the long side, tenderloin on the short. Flank and 95 percent lean ground beef are also good choices.

Whole baked chicken is a favorite at our house. Rub olive oil between the skin and meat and cook 45 minutes at 350° to an interior temperature of 165°. It will be clean, juicy, and not over-cooked. Pork tenderloin is lean and more affordable than steak. My doggies love the leftovers and rib bone. According to World Health Organization, bacon is in the same carcinogenesis category as tobacco because of cancer-causing nitrates. Broccoli is bacon of the veggie world. Broc on!

Seafood is more expensive but a very nutritious meat. According to *Seafood Watch*, the six healthiest fish are Albacore tuna, wild salmon, sole, mackerel, oysters, sardines, rainbow trout, and freshwater coho salmon. Fish to avoid are bluefin tuna, Chilean sea bass, grouper, monkfish, orange roughie, and farmed salmon. Sardines make the top ten of every healthy list but eating a fish that's staring back is only half the challenge. Covering those nasty critters with enough Louisiana hot sauce to blunt the taste is the other half. The benefits of seafood include omega-3, iron, vitamins B & D, and protein. Give a man a fish and he'll eat for a day; teach a man to fish and he'll sit in the boat and drink beer all day.

Eat at least one potassium-rich dish every day. The periodic table symbol "K" balances cell water levels and counteracts excess sodium. Foods rich in potassium include coffee, avocados, bananas, tomato juice, baked sweet potato, spinach, salmon, oranges, and cantaloupe.

Fats occur in two types—unsaturated is good; saturated is bad. Good (or smart) fats include extra virgin olive oil, avocados, almonds, pecans, pistachios, walnuts, hazelnuts, macadamia, chia, flax, pumpkin seeds, and fish oil. I take two fish oil pills (1200mg) each day. Saturated (bad) fats generally come from animal and dairy sources—butter, shortening, chicken skin, fried foods, cookies, and crackers. Use extra virgin olive oil or almond oil for high-heat cooking. Your lips will enjoy it as much as Aunt Hilda's bacon grease . . . without the lipids.

Fiber is important for regular bodily function. It regulates bowel movements, reduces cholesterol, and helps control blood sugar and weight. Some of the best fiber foods include freshly squeezed orange juice, Metamucil, pears, avocados, strawberries, raspberries, bananas, carrots, beets, broccoli, Brussel sprouts, lentils, split peas, chickpeas, quinoa, oats, almonds, steel-cut oatmeal, cereal, and celery. Middle age is when you choose your cereal for the fiber, not the toy.

In recent years I've made a conscious effort to chew food better. It contributes to eating less, satisfies hunger more, and encourages digestion. Small bites are better than large. Nutritionists recommend counting to thirty-two with each bite and chewing food until it loses its texture. Better chewing contributes to better nutrient utilization. The stomach's gastric juices have the task of reducing a big bite of sirloin to microscopic particles for entering the bloodstream. Your body is happier when the pearly whites simplify the tummy's job. Fast food gets the attention, but slow food gets the prize.

Sweat Is Fat Crying

In November 2020 I joined Planet Fitness. I had never lifted weights seriously one day in my life. I played sports in high school and made a few nominal trips to the weight room, but mostly as a spectator. My brain was programmed to auto-correct 'crunches' to 'cupcakes.' Starting now at age sixty-four? Would I be the laughingstock of the gym? I began reading body-building books and quickly realized its importance. According to Arnie Schwarz, "If it jiggles, it's fat. Muscles are made to be firm." Atrophy is not a trophy. Fifty years ago, a hospital patient would lie in bed for a couple of weeks to recover from major surgery, but now we know better. Healing is active, not passive. Physical therapy now gets its own PhD degree, something that didn't even exist thirty years ago.

Sweating removes toxins and boosts immunity. It also cools the body and regulates temperature. Don't be like the lady whose doctor said she needed more exercise. She squatted, twisted, twirled, jumped up and down, and sweated for nearly an hour. By the time she got her leotards on she was ready to sit down and have some chocolate.

There are 650 muscles in the body. The heart is the strongest and exercised only with aerobics. Even nursing homes now offer aerobic classes. It turns out physical exercise is more beneficial for the brain than Sunday's crossword puzzle. And nobody has laughed at me in Planet Fitness yet, at least not to my face. The sign on the wall says, "Judgment Free Zone." Thank goodness!

Aside from looking and feeling better, working out with weights increases the body's metabolism and allows more diet freedom. After lifting weights for one hour followed by twenty minutes of aerobics, it's time for a guilt-free feast of clean foods. Metabolism can stay elevated up to forty-eight hours, and muscles need forty-eight hours to recover and rebuild. Food is the most abused anxiety drug; exercise is the most underutilized antidepressant.

I have a personal list of foods that are beneficial for muscle-building and exercise recovery. It includes boiled egg, oatmeal, sweet potatoes, brown rice, quinoa, kidney beans, couscous, green peas, multigrain cereal, pumpkin seeds, sunflower seeds, chickpeas, bananas, blueberries, raspberries, almonds, avocado, lentils, raspberries, beets, and whole chicken. I also take vegan protein pills (20-25g, made from lentils) after a workout, and the protein packs near lunch meats in the grocery store are also great. Eat well so you'll look like you just stepped out of GQ instead of DQ.

Janet and I have learned that bike riding is our best aerobic exercise. We've tried jogging, walking, stationary biking, and treadmilling, but nothing works like street biking. Our weight looks best the morning after a brisk ride the day before. Maybe that's the key to long life in China, which has half a billion two-wheelers. Great minds think a bike. There are twice as many bikes on planet earth as cars. We subscribe to the notion that starts each day with a quick trip to the potty followed by a quick trip to the bathroom scales. A bike ride makes that second trip a little less frightening.

Body Mass Index (BMI) is a popular measure of physical health. The BMI value is a result of dividing weight by the square of height. A high BMI indicates high body fat. The following graph is helpful. My BMI is 22 at 5 feet, 11 inches, 160 lbs. which is in the green underweight. How about you? Check out the BMI chart below to see where you stand:

I Need More Vitamin Sea

"You must take a multivitamin." . . . "Vitamins are a waste." . . . "Take vitamin D to avoid Covid." . . . "Too much vitamin D causes cancer." Which is it? Who knows? The word *vitamin* comes from the words *vita*, which means *life*, and *amine* for amino acids. The derivation of vitamins is the original thought that the body needs more amino acids. Some vitamins cannot be synthesized by the body, so cells rely on plant/animal foods and supplements to maintain an adequate supply. I have taken a daily plant-based multivitamin for twenty years without side effects.

Vitamins C, D and beta-carotene (a form of vitamin A) act as antioxidants—preventing the body from oxygen damage. Vitamin A is important for vision and immunity. Spend time in the sun for Vitamin D and better bone health. Vitamin K aids blood clotting. Vitamins A, D, E, K are water soluble (removed by kidneys, become urine). "A Dog Eats Kidney" is an acrostically catchy way to remember those. They are believed to free up energy in food. It seems appropriate if you're on the Paleo diet that chewable Flintstones vitamins might be your best choice.

Official Sports Drink for Best Health

One of the best drugs is not found in a pill bottle but a water bottle. There is no greater gift for your body. Benefits from water include:

- Transports nutrients and oxygen to your cells.
- Flushes bacteria and toxins from your bladder and bloodstream.
- Aids digestion.
- Prevents constipation.
- Cushions joints.
- Regulates body temperature.
- Helps control calories.
- Energizes muscles.
- Improves the appearance of skin.
- Forms saliva and mucous.
- Helps regulate blood pressure.
- Helps with bowel function.

BMI Chart

Weight lbs →	100	105	110	115	120	125	130	135	140	145	150	155	160	165	170	175	180	185	190	195	200	205	210	215
Weight kgs →	45.5	47.7	50.0	52.3	54.5	56.9	59.1	61.4	63.6	65.9	68.2	70.5	72.7	75.0	77.3	79.5	81.8	84.1	86.4	88.6	90.9	93.2	95.5	97.7
Height in/cm ↓	Healthy						Overweight				Obese												Extremely Obese	
5'0" - 152.4	19	20	21	22	23	24	25	26	27	28	29	30	31	32	33	34	35	36	37	38	39	40	41	42
5'1" - 154.9	18	19	20	21	22	23	24	25	26	27	28	29	30	31	32	33	34	35	36	36	37	38	39	40
5'2" - 157.4	18	19	20	21	22	22	23	24	25	26	27	28	29	30	31	32	33	33	34	35	36	37	38	39
5'3" - 160.0	17	18	19	20	21	22	22	23	24	25	26	27	28	29	30	31	32	32	33	34	35	36	37	38
5'4" - 162.5	17	18	18	19	20	21	22	23	24	24	25	26	27	28	29	30	30	31	32	33	34	35	36	37
5'5" - 165.1	16	17	18	19	20	20	21	22	23	24	25	25	26	27	28	29	30	30	31	32	33	34	35	35
5'6" - 167.0	16	17	17	18	19	20	21	21	22	23	24	25	25	26	27	28	29	29	30	31	32	33	34	34
5'7" - 170.1	15	16	17	18	18	19	20	21	22	22	23	24	25	25	26	27	28	29	29	30	31	32	33	33
5'8" - 172.7	15	16	16	17	18	19	19	20	21	22	22	23	24	25	25	26	27	28	28	29	30	31	32	32
5'9" - 175.2	14	15	16	17	17	18	19	20	20	21	22	22	23	24	25	25	26	27	28	28	29	30	31	31
5'10" - 177.8	14	15	15	16	17	18	18	19	20	20	21	22	23	23	24	25	25	26	27	28	28	29	30	30
5'11" - 180.3	14	14	15	16	16	17	18	18	19	20	21	21	22	23	23	24	25	25	26	27	28	28	29	30
6'0" - 182.8	13	14	14	15	16	17	17	18	19	19	20	21	21	22	23	23	24	25	25	26	27	27	28	29
6'1" - 185.4	13	13	14	15	15	16	17	17	18	19	19	20	21	21	22	23	23	24	25	25	26	27	27	28
6'2" - 187.9	12	13	14	14	15	16	16	17	18	18	19	19	20	21	21	22	23	23	24	25	25	26	27	27
6'3" - 190.5	12	13	13	14	15	15	16	16	17	18	18	19	20	20	21	21	22	23	23	24	25	25	26	26
6'4" - 193.0	12	12	13	14	14	15	15	16	17	17	18	18	19	20	20	21	22	22	23	23	24	25	25	26

Underweight

www.free-printable-paper.com

Get the drift? We need water and sun—we're houseplants with emotions! Losing as little as 2% of body water can alter body temperature, reduce motivation, and increase fatigue. The body is 60% water with blood being 90% H2O. According to the CDC, men need four quarts daily, women three. Those recommendations seem like a lot but feasible during an entire day. Drink water at room temperature to avoid coughing.

Perhaps the most crucial need for water is brain function. Now I've got your attention. A 1-2% loss of body fluids after exercise impairs mood and concentration. Dehydration has also been shown to trigger headaches. Habits are hard to break, but when I realized the benefits of drinking water, I cut back on carbonated and sugary beverages. One of the best times to drink a couple glasses of water is after a meal as it helps produce digestive juices. Drinking a gallon of water each day helps avoid other people's drama because you're too busy going to the bathroom.

Less Obvious Doesn't Mean Less Painful

The first question my doctor asks at my annual checkup is, "Are you depressed?" My answer, "How can I be? I'm living my best life!" But we all know life can be tough. Depression costs our nation $210 billion annually. That's more than obesity. During years of ministry, I visited lots of depressed people. I would encourage them to stay active, open the curtains for more sunlight, open their life to more friends, and search for fun every day.

One in five Americans experience a mental health issue. Suicide is the second-leading cause of death among people ages 10-34 and ranks tenth overall. An amazing 70 percent of youth in juvenile detention centers have been diagnosed with mental illness, but only 44 percent seek treatment. The highest form of success is peace of mind and anything that costs that much is too expensive.

The psyche needs exercise just like the pecs. According to WebMD.com, exercise boosts feel-good chemicals called "endorphins" that encourage the brain to rewire itself in positive ways. Walking on the sidewalk is better than nothing. The online MD also encourages eating healthy foods and getting ample sleep. If you're an old man and it makes you happy to walk around the block with your suspenders holding your pants up around your nipples, go for it.

According to *Prevention* magazine, the MIND diet can turn back cognitive aging. MIND stands for Mediterranean Intervention for Neurodegenerative

Delay. It is rich in leafy greens, berries, nuts, fish, and olive oil, much like the Mediterranean Diet. More than 900 men and women with an average age 81.4 detailed their diets and underwent a cognitive assessment over a four-year period. By following the diet along with limiting red meats, sugary treats, and fried foods, they cut Alzheimer's risk by 53 percent. That's an eye-opening stat! Diet is like an investment account; healthy food choices pay rich dividends.

Sleep Number Is One

Good sleep is essential for good health is. Everybody has their biological sleep number and mine is seven hours. I'm not sure the air chambers in the mattress (which determine the sleep number of a mattress) make much of a difference. According to health.gov, sleep helps the body fight disease, manage weight control, reduce stress, and enhance social interaction. A lack of sleep causes the body to release cortisol, a stress hormone that makes the heart work harder. I've never understood why it's called beauty sleep when we wake up looking like a troll!

I'm hopelessly a morning person, so I'm disgustingly an early-to-bed person. 8:05 P.M. is past my bedtime. 5:05 A.M. is past my wakeup time. When I get to be world czar, I'm doing away with daylight savings time and enacting reverse daylight savings time by adding an extra hour of sun to mornings!

The good Lord rested on the Sabbath, and it's the only day He blessed. Your body is created for resting and blessing. Like a car getting new spark plugs, rest fine tunes the body mentally and physically. A baseball starting pitcher throws only every five days so his arm can rest. Bodybuilders rest forty-eight hours between workouts so muscles can recover. A day of rest is also a blessing for the soul. We're made for mental healing through reflection and rebooting. I wish I could have followed this principle more in my life. There are seven days in a week and someday isn't one of them.

Random facts at 5:06 A.M. . . . humans spend one-third of their life asleep; cats spend two-thirds. A giraffe needs only a couple of hours of sleep each day. The Guinness record for longest period a human went without sleep is eleven days. Twelve percent of the population dream in black and white. Those born blind experience dreams involving emotions, sound, and smell rather than sight. Some 15 percent of the population are sleepwalkers—with the favorite destination being the fridge. Sleeping on the stomach aids digestion; another liability of pregnancy. Caterpillars have it figured out—eat a lot, sleep a while, and wake up beautiful! Research shows that although one in four couples sleep in separate beds, sleeping next to someone you love makes you fall asleep faster, reduces depression, and promotes long life. If that's the case, I'll be a very old man!

Tooth Be Told . . . Floss is Boss

Good dental health is an often-neglected essential. It's expensive, and dental insurance has little value. As a licensed agent, I've encountered people who had a $500 per month car payment but hadn't driven to a dentist in ten years. Twenty-five percent of adults don't brush twice a day which increases tooth decay by 33 percent. Brush at night to keep your teeth. Brush in the morning to keep your friends.

Tooth prints are like fingerprints, unique to each person. If you don't floss, you're neglecting 40 percent of the tooth's surface. In a lifetime a person produces 100,000 gallons of saliva. That's enough to fill twenty semi-trucks! No wonder there's never been a cure-all like Mama's spit! There are more bacteria in your mouth than people living in the world. Right-handed people tend to chew food on the right side of the mouth, left-handed on the left. A woman smiles an average of sixty-eight times a day, men eight times. A smile is a curve that sets everything straight.

Bad to the Bone

Be wary of doctors recommending surgery. You have only one precious body, and surgery is always a major invasion. A *USA Today* survey indicated 10-20 percent of surgeries are unnecessary. The top unnecessary surgeries are pacemaker, back/spine, knee/hip, and hysterectomy. I've read about doctors leaving surgical tools in patients. One Vietnamese man was sewn up with a pair of scissors in his belly and lived with them eighteen years. Sign seen in bone and joint clinic, "It's going tibia great day!"

The body has an amazing ability to heal itself. Cells immediately start the healing process when sickness arrives. They also replicate to replace the destroyed or damaged ones. If you break a bone, the body quickly begins producing new cells to heal the damage. When your skin is cut, blood platelets begin clotting to stop the bleeding, white blood cells remove the dead, injured cells, and new healthy cells repair the damaged tissue. When we're exhausted at the end of a long day, our body heals itself with sleep.

A few years ago, Janet was having issues with lethargy (mostly because we had two kids in college and she was working hard), so she made an appointment with a doctor. He recommended major thyroid surgery which included oral medication for the rest of her life and a scar on her neck. She decided to give it time for observation to give the body a chance to heal itself. After a couple months she felt better and has never had another thyroid issue. Her blood numbers have been perfect for several annual checkups. Be especially wary when doctors schedule surgery on the 1st or 15th of the month! A sign on a lady's medical clinic, 'If life gives you lemons, a simple operation can give you melons.'

An annual checkup is the best prevention for unnecessary surgery. My mother and grandmother were both diagnosed with cancer in their fifties, but it was discovered at their annual checkup and removed with surgery. The amount of data available in a simple blood draw is astonishing, even though nine out of ten blood draws are in vein. The health of kidneys, lungs, liver, urinary tract, skin, heart, prostate, and thyroid can be assessed, as well as levels of cholesterol, vitamins, folic acid, and calcium. Ignorance is not bliss when it comes to the body because knowledge is power for better health.

Just Takes One Bad Apple

Janet and I recently visited France. The people are slimmer than Americans and their diets are generally healthier, but smoking is rampant. That bad habit has been lessened in our country in recent years, but not in France. The trip reminded me of the need to care for the whole person—to check all the benchmarks. You may eat the best food and go to bed hungry every night, but smoking a pack of cigarettes a day negates it all. It's also one of the most expensive habits. One pack a day wastes $250 per month. Smokers reduce their lifespan by eleven minutes per cigarette.

While we were in France, Queen Elizabeth II died. She was the second-longest reigning monarch in world history with seventy years on the throne. French King Louis XIV reigned seventy-two years.

In a recent interview, the queen gave her twelve rules for healthy living:

- Never stop learning, keep your brain active.
- Tackle one task at a time with full concentration (vs. multitasking).
- Establish a strong sense of purpose for your life.
- Designate plenty of time for fun and play.
- Develop routines for each day.
- Reward yourself with an occasional dessert or drink.

- Select exercises you enjoy.
- Don't trouble yourself too much about being liked.
- Embrace getting older.
- Take regular breaks/vacations.
- Don't let life's drama get you down.
- Be kind to everyone.

The queen also had a beautiful sense of humor. When walking the grounds of Balmoral with her protection officer, she ran into some American tourists. It became clear they didn't recognize her: "Have you ever met the queen?" they shouted. "No," she responded, and then pointed at her protection officer. "But he has."

Some parting trivials (if that's a word):

- Laughing a hundred times is equivalent to fifteen minutes on the stationary bike.
- We burn more calories sleeping than watching television.
- Right-handed people live on average nine years longer than left-handed people.
- We are one-centimeter taller in the morning than in the evening.
- Motorists who drive and talk on a cell phone are more impaired than drunk drivers with blood alcohol of .08.

When visiting Paris one of the first observations is no yellow or white traffic lines on the downtown streets. It's every man for himself. It results in lots of horns and fingers. Some people look at physical health like those streets. Just get in your body and drive with no lines. But your life's trip will be safer, longer, and with fewer honks if you stay within some lines.

The first benchmark of success is physical health. It's impossible to be very happy if you are very hurting. Nurturing self is not selfish, but self-preserving. If you treat your body like a temple, it will worship you. Health is the best hobby. Arnie got this one right!

"When someone said, 'I never want to look like you.' I said, 'Don't worry, you never will.'"
— **Arnold Schwarzenegger**

2

THE SOCIAL

W E ARE CREATED TO LIVE OUR LIVES WITH OTHER LIVES. The word *together* is found five hundred times in the Bible. Adam was lonely and needed a mate. God created Eve because He knew Adam wanted a mate. It's fun to enjoy the breeze on a fall front porch, but it's more fun to enjoy a friend and shoot the breeze. Our lives are incomplete without friends and family.

Animals are also social creatures, and we classify them by their companionships. A swarm of bees, herd of cows, colony of rats, covey of quail, drove of turkeys, and my favorite, pride of lions. A pod of dolphins teams up to herd a school of fish toward the shore so they'll be easier prey. I have a Purple Martin birdhouse in my backyard. They live together in colonies and enjoy being near humans. The guiltiest moment of my day is the sad look on my toy poodle's face when I leave her to be alone. The little emotional manipulator!

Studies have shown that brains grow and thrive with social interaction. Our first relationship was with Mom. Nurturing and cuddling enhance cognitive development. Participating in social activities is exercise for the brain just as treadmill is exercise for the body. It produces better blood flow and improves hypothalamus function. What lady doesn't feel better after a 'girls' night out' party?

Social Is a Good Word

English is the only language with words that have multiple meanings. The word *set* has 430 meanings in the Oxford English Dictionary. Because *social* is a derivative of *society*, the terms *socialism, socialist, social justice*, and *social reform* have become headline words. The connotations have dampened the word in today's world.

When John F. Kennedy was assassinated in 1963, President Lyndon B. Johnson started the so-called Great Society. This included social welfare, Social Security, Medicare, Medicaid, and other social initiatives. With sympathy for the Kennedy family running high, a Democrat majority was elected to Congress in 1964. They ratified those social initiatives.

In 1950, national expenditure in the federal budget for social proposals was less than 10 percent. But by 2022, our expenditures for Social Security, Medicare, Medicaid, Obamacare, and other social ascendancies have increased to 55 percent. And much of it has been funded with artificial (printed) money. More on that later. Entitlement programs account for more national spending than all other federal government programs combined.

The federal debt has grown from around $380 billion in 1960 to $31 trillion in 2022. Payment on debt interest alone is 12 percent of our federal budget. Our nation's debt to gross domestic product ratio has increased from 40 percent in 1964 to 130 percent in 2022. One of my main motivations for authoring this book is to give my grandchildren tips for a successful life. It's troubling that they'll inherit a $31 trillion national debt. The great society of the past fifty years has done them a great injustice.

Friendship Is Underrated Medication

The point of this chapter is that *social* is still a good word and at least one-fourth of a successful life. Society is like a large piece of frozen water where skating well is the great art of social life. Rudolph Steiner: "A healthy social life is found when, in the mirror of each soul, the whole community finds its reflection, and when, in the whole community, the virtue of each one is living." Nothing energizes the psyche more than the chemistry of a close friend. Food for the psyche is as important as food for the body.

The appearance of social life can be misleading. Lady Gaga has fame and fortune. She built a net worth of $150 million by age thirty-four and sells out concerts all over the world. But she lamented, "I'm alone every night. All these people will leave, right? They will leave and then I'll be alone. And

I go from everyone touching me all day and talking to me, to total silence." She wants to remain single because she thinks marriage will take away her artistic creativity. If she only knew!

Madonna, the Material Girl, has grossed $1.5 billion in concert revenue and has a net worth of $850 million, but she's been through three marriages and lost custody of her son. She said recently, "There were whole chunks of my life when I was so lonely. I felt like I didn't have a friend in the world." I'll never understand how Hollywood has become so hallowed in America.

Robin Williams was one of Hollywood's favorites. Funny, brilliant, and oozing with charisma. His movie, *Mrs. Doubtfire*, was the number-two box office movie in the world in 1993. I remember driving by the house in San Francisco where it was filmed. By 2014 his net worth had swelled to $50 million, but he felt all alone due to medical diagnoses. He committed suicide in the middle of the night, hanging himself with his own belt. Loneliness leads to depression which can lead to disaster.

According to one study, loneliness is as bad for health as smoking fifteen cigarettes a day and decreases life expectancy by 26 percent. High blood pressure, depression, stroke, and cognitive decline are symptoms of an unhealthy social life. Other than the death penalty, the worst punishment in our prison system is solitary confinement. Being alone 23 hours a day 365 days a year might be worse than death.

A *YouGov* survey found that 20 percent of Americans have no close friends. I knew a lady in my hometown who died and wasn't found for over a week. Nobody missed her in seven days! Yes, Howard Hughes was the richest man in the world, but no, he wasn't happy. The money doesn't matter if we don't matter to others.

Research indicates people make about four hundred friends in a lifetime. Men tend to maintain an intimate relationship with only a few people while women cast a larger net. According to a Switzerland study of two hundred college freshmen, those who developed more friends made better grades. Looking back on my college days, the students who were leaders of their social clubs have been more successful in life.

Whether doctor, lawyer, salesperson, or name one, social skills equal success. I chose my doctor partly because he is well educated and has a good reputation, but also because I like him and can talk to him. A tele-salesperson with a grin in her voice has a better chance. And I'm more inclined to go back to a restaurant if the server smiles and gives me free bread.

My son worked as a waiter at Cheesecake Factory while attending college. This restaurant attracts professional waiters who make a generous living. Carson was just part-time, after classes, and on weekends.

One day I needed his signature on an insurance form. We scheduled our meeting for the breakroom at Cheesecake. While waiting for him, I noticed the waiters were listed on the whiteboard in order of their income for the previous week. I was surprised to see Carson's name on top. I asked how that happened. How did he make more money than the professional waiters who worked more hours?

He said the restaurant has a script for the waiters to use when they approach a table. It pushes appetizers and the most expensive menu items... and annoys the patrons. "I just go to their table and treat them like a million bucks; get to know them and serve them to the max with sweet tea and free bread." He continued, "I smile at them and usually tell them I'm a student at Lipscomb University. They like me and give me a better tip." Social skills bring financial success. Carson has always been a people person and it has served him well.

The Best, Best Friend

While Janet and I were visiting the Eiffel Tower in Paris, France, our guide told us the structure was completed in 1889 to coincide with the start of the World's Fair. It was completed in just two years, and nobody died in construction. But after completion, one worker took his girlfriend to the second level and proposed marriage. When she accepted, he got so excited he lost his balance and fell to his tragic death. I guess love really can be a fatal attraction.

The richest social life we can experience is with a spouse. I'm blessed that my wife is my best friend. We've been together almost every day since we were sixteen years old. We grew up together and now we're growing old together. It's a true saying—happy is a man who finds a true friend and far happier is he who finds that true friend in his wife. The Roman poet Horace was the first to coin the words *better half.* Janet and I are a perfect fit because she's my better half. If I could pass along only one social legacy to my grandchildren, it would be a successful marriage. Not just a long marriage, but a loving marriage.

I went to a weekend church retreat in October 1974 which included a Friday night hayride. Those wouldn't be exciting enough for today's kids, but fall hayrides were a rite of autumn in my little town. By God's grace, I sat on a bale beside a beauty from Bon Aqua. I'd never met her but knew she was the junior class candidate for high school homecoming queen.

I found the courage to ask her for a date the following weekend. Dad let me borrow his brand-new black 1974 Chevrolet Caprice. I wouldn't have shined a Rolls Royce any brighter. We started dating every weekend and she lived 20 miles from my house. Most of our dates ended up back in Centerville. That's 20 miles out to Bon Aqua, 20 back, 20 back-out, and 20 home... or 80 miles per date. We dated five years before we were married. That's about 50,000 miles, but I would have driven around the world for this girl! My grandfather bought me a green 1972 Buick Skylark with an 8-track cassette player which hosted most of our dates. I owned every Fleetwood Mac cartridge.

She was usually late, I was usually (always) early which is painful for a Mr. Prompt. I got really acquainted with her dad. Like Jacob and Rachel in the Bible, our chats during the wait became an added bride price. My edge on him, however, was that he was near retirement and wanted the last one off his meal ticket.

Ona Rodgers, a family friend of my childhood, oft reminded me that happiness in this life and the one to come depends on the one I married. I've surely found that to be true. Janet is the mother of my children and the love of my life. And yes, she was crowned 1974 HCHS homecoming queen. The number one key to my success is my number-one friend. We're better together!

According to the *Guinness Book of World Records,* Herbert and Zelmyra Fisher had the longest recorded marriage at eighty-six years. Zelmyra said, "He is my friend for life; our marriage has lasted a lifetime." When asked for the secret she said, "Respect, support, and communicate with each other. Be faithful, honest, and true. Love each other with all your heart." There is no better life than being married to your best friend. It's the heart of success!

At this writing, George & Doreen Kirby were the oldest couple to get married. They were 103 and 91, respectively. He proposed on Valentine's Day and then posted on Facebook, "I'm told the Guinness Book of Records has officially acknowledged Doreen and I will be the oldest couple in the world to marry. Who would have thought it? I need to lie down to think about it more." Every ear yearns for those sweetest words—*I love you.* George died just before their first anniversary with the words forever ringing in his heart.

We have a man at church I began observing recently. He and his wife are senior citizens, but it's obvious he dearly loves her. I've noticed him opening her car door and he sits with his arm around her at church. I noticed him giving her a gentle kiss one Sunday. She smiles a lot and so does he. She is always dressed impeccably and gently raises her hands to worship the Lord.

I recently became aware she's struggling with early stages of dementia, and I had no idea. It hasn't changed the way her husband treats or loves her. Perhaps enhanced it. There's nothing like love that lasts a lifetime. It's the heart of social life.

Model Social Life

I've always admired the social habits of the African-American community. It's clear they love each other and enjoy spending time together. Martin Luther King, Jr., "We must learn to live together as brothers or perish as fools." Drive through their neighborhoods and they're sitting on the front porch talking, standing on the back porch cooking, or playing pickup basketball in the driveway. Their social unity is their strength.

According to various sources (not me), the world's best food is India; best coffee is Colombia; best diamonds are Botswana; best education system is Denmark; most woman-per-man ratio is Estonia; most sheep is New Zealand; fastest download speed is Romania; most man-per-woman ratio is United Arab Emirates; most Miss Universes is Venezuela; most doughnuts is Canada; most healthy is Singapore; but best social community is African American.

A Mind Reader

I enjoy social media. I've reconnected with friends through Facebook I wouldn't have thought about again in my life. I have FB friends from elementary school days who hadn't crossed my mind in fifty years. Now we're keeping up every day. I have Facebook friends I met many years ago, friends I met a few years ago, and friends I've never met. I have friends who are talkers and friends who are stalkers; friends who are political and friends who are polite. I have friends who are Vandy fans, and a few Vols have slipped in. I enjoy them all and start every morning with a cup of coffee and a slice of Facebook. As a child, I wondered what it would be like to read minds, then I got a Facebook account.

I enjoy Facebook funnies. A woman posts, "I was in Walmart buying a bag of Purina Dog Chow when the lady behind me asks if I have a dog?

Duh?? Why else would I be buying dog food? I said, 'No, I started the Purina Diet again, but I shouldn't because last time I ended up in the intensive care unit at the hospital. But I lost fifty pounds. It's a perfect diet. All you do is fill your pockets with Purina nuggets and when you're hungry, pop one in your mouth.' The wide-eyed lady replied, 'But did the dog food poison you? Is that why you ended up in intensive care?' 'Oh no,' I replied, 'I stepped off the curb to sniff a poodle's butt and a car hit me.'"

In February 2004, a Harvard sophomore, Mark Zuckerberg, created a website called Facemash. It was a place for students to compare female faces and decide who's the hottest on campus. The site was shut down by the administration and Zuckerberg was threatened with expulsion. He then created an online student directory called theFacebook where students could find out who was taking the same classes and enjoy an online social network. The 'the' was eventually dropped, but the lawsuit from three students from whom he stole the idea was not. Mark eventually paid them $65 million and stock in the company. At this writing, his net worth is $52 billion.

An astounding 71 percent of Americans have a Facebook page; 2.5 billion worldwide. Only half of Facebookers speak English. When we were in France, businesses were asking patrons to follow them on Facebook. The blue "F" on the restaurant cheque was about the only thing I could read . . . merci! Senior citizens are the fastest-growing segment with 60 percent of baby boomers having an account. The two most active times are 8 A.M. and 10 P.M., and 75 percent visit daily. The average FB time spent per person is an incredible fifty-eight minutes a day. Stalking is all fun and games until you accidentally hit the Like button. Guilty of all the above!

Follow me on Facebook: "Larry Rogers." I love new friends. Beware: many pics of grandkids and more bad jokes.

YouTube is the second most popular social media site. It was started in May 2005 by three former employees of PayPal. The first video was uploaded by founder Jawed Karim of "A Day at the Zoo." Now a phenomenal 1.8 billion users upload 500 hours of data every minute and generate $15 billion annual revenue. YouTube is an American-only social media. The all-time most-viewed video is *Baby Shark Dance*, a stat contributed by my granddaughter. She loves that little jingle! Husband to wife, "Of course I can do your hair. I took online classes at YouTube University and interned at Pinterest." The answers to life's handyperson and honey-do dilemmas are now just a click away. If my pesty "change oil" light won't turn off, it's off to YouTube for the instructions!

An irony of loneliness is "many people" doesn't necessarily lead to many friends. An individual in New York City can be surrounded by ten million bodies but not one buddy. Friendly and friend are derivatives but not synonyms. The big city can be big seclusion. Loneliness is not being alone but the feeling no one cares.

Tips for making a friend in a large city (or anywhere) include join a church, volunteer, join an exercise class, visit a coffee shop, walk the dog, add new Facebook friends, join a gym, sign up for an exercise class, become a master gardener, and/or do something out of your comfort zone. Others are also searching for you. Make yourself available. Everybody wants more friends. To the world you may be one person, but to one person you may be the world. Making friends is the purest form of reciprocity. You make one when you are one; receive when you give. The golden rule always rules.

Forgiveness Is for the Strong

Billy Graham was one of my heroes. His autobiography, *Just As I Am*, is a must-read. Dad took me to a crusade at Vanderbilt Stadium in June 1979. Dr. Graham was a friend to all. He taught, "The Bible teaches us to be more concerned about the needs and feelings of others than our own. We are to encourage and build self-confidence in our loved ones, friends, and associates." He was a social genius.

My dad was also a well-known pastor who served on the board of directors at Lipscomb University fifteen years. One night our family was eating in a restaurant when a man stopped at our table. He looked at Dad, "I think I know you, but I can't think of your name." Dad smiled a little. "Yes, I've seen you on TV. I'm racking my brain." Dad blushed a little more. "Wait, it just hit me. I know who you are... you're Billy Graham!!" They did bear a strong resemblance. We had a good laugh!

If you watched Dr. Graham's funeral, you know it was a beautiful eulogy given by his children. That's every man's dream. We all want our children to respect and love us, especially as we get older. I was particularly intrigued by the eulogy of his daughter, Ruth.

She began her remarks by saying she always considered herself to be the black sheep of the family. She divorced after twenty years of marriage. She said, "I was so disappointed in myself. I just wanted to hide. And then, my family all told me not to marry anyone else quickly, but being an all-wise person, wiser than anybody in the family, I didn't need their counsel.

I married again in just a few months and that marriage also ended quickly, due to abuse.

"I felt like I had not only let myself down but had also embarrassed the great Billy Graham. I just couldn't bear to face him and didn't see him for several weeks," she continued. "But then one day I decided to contact him. I sheepishly told him I wanted to come visit. I was so nervous about what he'd say.

"I got in my car and began driving from near the West Coast all the way to the Black Mountains of North Carolina. With each mile, my blood pressure increased. It was a long drive. I just couldn't imagine how disappointed he must be.

"I finally made it to Montreat. Our driveway winds back and forth up the steep mountain and with each turn my palms were a little sweatier. By the time I reached that last curve, I was trembling. But then I looked up and standing in the middle of the road with his arms wide open... it was my Daddy. Smiling as he ran to my car to greet me.

"'I love you so much, Ruth. Your Mom and I are excited you're here. She's been cooking for a week. Come on in. We can't wait to spend some time with you!'"

A word that sustains a friendship is *forgiveness*. For some reason it's easier to forgive our enemies than our friends. But just as a broken bone is stronger after it mends, a friendship is stronger after it heals. Forgiveness is a win-win—relationship is salvaged, and a forgiver is salved. Forgiveness doesn't mean ignoring the pain but deciding the pain won't control your life.

The teachings of Jesus are countercultural. He forgave the people who were considered the worst of sinners—those who needed it most. What a novel idea! The Law of Moses prescribed severe penalties for those transgressions. But Jesus knew nobody could keep all those rules. Sabbath Day laws banned such activities as cooking, gathering wood, and buying 'n selling. And the Pharisees added 613 more *Shabbat* rules making it unlawful to set a broken bone, remove a dead corpse from rubble, or walk more than 1,999 paces on that day.

Jesus came to bring a new life, a life of new forgiveness. We are fallen and make mistakes. We tend toward sin and often succumb. But because of forgiveness we become a new creation, old things pass away. And just as He forgives us, we forgive others. Living life with a clear conscience is the fruit of a forgiving heart.

I remember hearing news of the massacre of small children at a one-room Amish schoolhouse in Nickel Mines, Pennsylvania on October 2, 2006. Charles Roberts, the local milkman, shot ten girls, killing five before turning the gun on himself. It was one of the most senseless, heinous crimes anyone could imagine. The whole nation was outraged.

How did the Amish respond? Within just a couple of hours they went to Roberts's widow's house expressing their sympathy and forgiveness. A few days later, the majority of those attending the killer's graveside funeral arrived in horse-drawn buggies. And a year later the Amish made a financial donation to the widow and her three children. To some people, their forgiveness seems as senseless as the killer's actions, but to forgive is to set a captive free and realize the captive is you.

Several of the biggest mistakes in my life have been due to a lack of forgiveness. I'm thinking of a church I was pastoring, a church I dearly loved. Most Monday mornings an elder would come to my office to point out what I had done wrong the previous Sunday. He wanted me to be more critical of the beliefs of other denominations. That had never been my style and I wasn't comfortable serving as final judge. It eventually cost me my job, but I could have handled it with more forgiveness.

A warm social life keeps forgiveness on the front burner. It's not our natural response, but the way to victory for our fallen nature. Jesus was counter-cultural in order for us to forgive when it seems senseless. I wonder how many marriages would be saved if forgiveness was in the house? How many fewer inmates? Less lonely people?

You Are Only You

A five-word key for healthy social living is "Find what works for you." You don't have to hit the club every night to make friends. If you don't like football games, that's not your hangout. Ask yourself—*Where am I comfortable with people? Where do I find those who share my interests?*

I know a group of retired teachers who have lunch every few weeks. They have a common interest and enjoy each other. When I was a pastor, I planned monthly social outings for our senior citizens. The group loved each other and enjoyed the day. My grandmother was a farmer's wife who didn't have many opportunities to socialize, but she was a member of the local home demonstration club forty years. It was her people. I lived on a street with a group of ladies who enjoyed quilting. They got together each week to *sewcialize* (sorry).

When Janet and I had young children, we networked with other parents at school and church who had children of similar age. It was what worked for us during that phase of our lives. Now we're networking with grandparents who have similar grandchildren. I recently visited some independent living centers with Mom. The tours emphasized the social opportunities available for residents—a secret of success at any age.

Having a common interest makes icebreaking easier. Keep the first interactions brief. Look for opportunities to network. The first person you meet might not always be the one. Be a source of positive energy and happiness. Keep a few upbeat conversation starters in mind. Say yes to the ask.

Perfection Is Imperfect

One thing that challenges my social skills is perfectionism. Webster defines it as a personal standard, attitude, or philosophy that demands perfection and rejects anything less. According to my wife, my closet is alphabetized! Not exactly, but my shirts are sorta color coded. Perfectionists have an inner voice telling them they're not good enough, demanding personal relationships at the top of the social circle. I have learned the more I let go, the higher I rise. The goal is progress, not perfection, and remember 90 percent is still an "A" and an occasional "B" isn't the end of the world. Social lives are richer when perfectionism is poorer. Bubba said he's a perfectionist and procrastinator—he wants his house to be perfect tomorrow.

A healthy social life gives self-confidence, and the capacity of your life is determined by your confidence. Money means self-assurance but good friends provide long-term value. They're like relatives you make for yourself. Having a friend to take a bullet is not as important as having one to take a bullet out of you. Best friends soothe the soul.

Land of the Happy

The *World Happiness Report* rates countries with the happiest people. The primary reason for that happiness is often a keen sense of community and family. Costa Rica is a perennial front runner. They're very communal, spend time outdoors, and eat a fresh and natural diet. The nation's slogan is *pura vida* which means *pure living*. In Iceland, 98 percent of residents know someone on whom they can rely in time of need. Neither of those would be considered the wealthiest nations, but they're happy because they love each other.

Finland is another Scandinavian country on the happy list. Their national philosophy is *lagom*, which means *just the right amount* or don't try to keep up with the Joneses. Norway has happiness rooted in their love of spending time together in the great outdoors. My hiking friend, Tom Beckwith, would enjoy living there and he also enjoys cool weather. Israel is on the list with their excellent diet and endearing Jewish family relationships. They like fruits, vegetables, mangos, melons, chickpeas, tomatoes, and cucumber salad. The benchmarks of success complement each other.

According to Gallup's *2019 Positive Experience Index*, Paraguay is the most "smiling, laughing, and displaying happiness" country on the planet. They believe happy feelings follow happy behavior. Prescription leads to description in much of life, especially the social side.

Social Booster Shots

I close the chapter with ten social booster shots. These rules have worked for me and will help you if you either have an obstacle to overcome or more friends than Tom Cruise.

Rule No. 1: Block self-pity completely. Wallowing, blaming, and justifying are excuses that let negativity win. All depression is rooted in self-pity. It's a form of living suicide. Never let that voice have ears!

Rule No. 2: Put yourself in situations where you thrive. Social success does not mean being comfortable in every social situation. If you have two left feet, the dance floor is not for you. Find your niche and tango.

Rule No. 3: Focus on the positive and surround yourself with positive people. You'll never have a fulfilling relationship with negative people. Everyone wants friends who are real, but being both real and positive is achievable.

Rule No. 4: Master good eye contact. Your eyes are the window of your soul. Practice eye contact and master it. Look straight ahead and avoid glancing at people who are staring at you. Worlds change when eyes meet.

Rule No. 5: Pay attention to your body language. Stand or sit up straight and move slowly. Appear relaxed and open to conversation. Psychologists say 50 percent of communication occurs through body posture.

Rule No. 6: Stay up to date on current events. Avoid topics that are controversial but be ready to offer something of interest, with humor. Most news is negative so plucking a few positive nuggets is a breath of fresh air.

Rule No. 7: Leave your phone in the car. Talking to someone who is pre-occupied by their phone is called *phubbing*. I guess there's a word for everything! I like cell phones, but when the call was tied to the wall with a wire, we had more social freedom.

Rule No. 8: Smile. It seems like a simple thing but it's everything. We're all attracted to a smile. It's free therapy and the shortest distance between two people. When you see someone without a smile, give them one of yours.

Rule No. 9: Initiate conversation. It puts people at ease. Don't be a counter puncher, but a discussion starter. It puts you in control. Avoid starting a conversation with a closed-loop question that only has the answer "yes."

Rule No. 10: Don't take yourself too seriously. Nobody else does. Keep conversations light and easy. It will make people take you more seriously. When you learn to accept instead of expect, you'll have fewer disappointments.

Someone said life is like drawing a picture without an eraser. That's especially true with social life. You can't change a thing that happened yesterday, but you can learn from mistakes and build relationships today for tomorrow. It's easy to reflect on a previous day and begrudge the things you'd like to take back, but it's better to block those thoughts and focus on the positives of today.

Success is not real unless it's whole, and it's not whole unless your body, soul, and spirit are mingled with others. Adam needed a friend. And you see in this chapter that physical well-being plays a part in social well-being. The benchmarks of success complement each other. That's the beauty of real success. Did you mentally file a "Barber clipping?"

At a church I pastored there was an elderly lady who had a problem with her neck. Her head was so bent over that her chin nearly touched her chest. She couldn't raise her head. It was a sad situation. I asked someone what happened. They said she lives alone in a rough neighborhood and fears for her life every night. She pushes a chair against the front door for double security and sleeps in the chair with her head bent over. She has done it for so long it has caused permanent damage to her neck.

She sat alone at church and didn't seem to have any friends. I often wondered if anybody ever really loved her. I saw it as my mission to befriend her. And love her. Whenever I was in her neighborhood, I'd stop for a short visit and prayer. Why? Partly because it thrilled her so much, but mostly because it energized me so much. She needed a friend and so did I. I took her a dozen doughnuts one day. She thought she'd hit the lotto. Social is the ultimate reciprocal. I look forward to seeing her again someday . . . in a place where doughnuts have zero calories and neighborhoods have many friends.

The second benchmark for success is a rich social life. It's the energy for a successful day. Elvis got this one right.

"Before you marry a person, you should first make them use a computer with really slow Internet to see who they really are."
— **Will Ferrell**

3

THe WEALTH

T HEY SAY MONEY DOESN'T MAKE YOU HAPPY; I say neither does being broke. The No. 1 best-selling self-help book of all-time is *Think and Grow Rich* by Napoleon Hill . . . and for good reason. It's impossible for the benchmarks of success to complement each other if the ends aren't meeting. The third benchmark for success is wealth.

When Janet and I got married in 1979, we took our honeymoon to Daytona Beach. We came back to a rented Nashville duplex and could count a grand total of $50 that was ours. We were so broke that first winter we turned off the heat on some frigid nights. We've laughed later about waking up to a thin skim of ice in the toilet. When spring arrived, we were even broker and hocked our prized class rings for $300. Someone said dead broke is the actual root of all evil. I can tell you firsthand that ain't far wrong.

We live in a society that requires much money for much living. You might be the most frugal person in town, but Kroger and United Healthcare don't care. You might have taken a virtual vow of poverty and live in a little house on the prairie, but diapers being on sale is a rarity. Inflation might have reduced your bucket list to a Dixie cup, but a shopping spree to *Everything's a Dollar* is now *Five Below*.

Money Memoirs

Hundreds of years ago people were more agrarian. T-bone steaks ate free pasture, pork chops ate homegrown corn, and the produce section was in the backyard. A horse and buggy didn't need Kroger points to afford a fill-up. Those were the days when GPS was a fencepost on the other side of the field and tan lines looked like you were wearing a shirt.

Thousands of years ago people used the barter system. Mesopotamian tribes were probably the first, six thousand years ago. Animal skins, salt, weapons, spices, and other goods were traded with much haggling. One negative of the barter system was that a go-between person was required to complete the transaction. If you wanted to kill a wooly mammoth with twelve-foot tusks and were bartering for an axe, you had to find a third party who thought that was a good idea. One of the benefits of introducing cash into society was increasing the speed of a financial transaction.

Apparently the first minted coins used as official currency were in Asia Minor (Turkey and surrounding area) circa 650 BC. The Greek poet Xenophanes quoted Herodotus, who said the Lydians were "the first to strike and use gold and silver coins." According to scholars, the Lydian stater is the oldest known coin. You can see one at the Metropolitan Museum of Art in New York City (the MET).

The first paper money was introduced by the Chinese in the 1200s. Venetian merchant Marco Polo visited China in 1271 and wrote of how "the Chinese emperor has a handle on both the money supply and its various denominations." Those first bills had the inscription, "Those who counterfeit will be beheaded." I'm glad cooler heads prevailed in our country with "In God We Trust."

In December 1690, a failed attack on Quebec and subsequent near mutiny forced the Massachusetts Bay Colony to issue the first paper currency in the Western Hemisphere. Then after the American Revolutionary War began in 1775, Continental Congress began issuing paper money known as *Continentals*. The first U.S. coins were struck in 1793 at the Philadelphia Mint and presented to Martha Washington. The motto on the coin was "Mind Your Business." Ben Franklin suggested the motto which didn't mean 'Stay out of my business,' but concentrate on your affairs and you will prosper.

The U.S. government didn't issue official paper money until 1861. They were called greenbacks and printed to pay for the Civil War. Today a $1,000 Confederate greenback is worth $35,000. And during a three-week period of our nation's history between December 1934 and January 1935, $100,000 bills were printed. There were only 42,000 printed, and they were designed for transactions between the Federal Reserve and Treasury. Those things are each worth $1.6 mill today. The U.S. Treasury Department could use a few!

Some of the biggest changes in money have occurred in the twenty-first century with mobile payments and virtual currency. Credit card machines and smart phones have mostly eliminated the need for paper money. The release of Bitcoin in 2009 was the first decentralized, non-government form of currency. The Bahamas rolled out the world's first digital currency, with China, Japan, and Sweden testing the waters.

The only money in my pocket is a money clip with four credit cards, one driver's license, my health cards, and the all-important Covid vaccination record. When we were in San Francisco in 2021, restaurants had bouncers stationed at the front door checking for proof. Yes, I also have pics of my granddaughters! If I need cash, an ATM machine is not far. Just wondering . . . but if the "M" in ATM stands for machine, why do we still say ATM machine?

The point of this chapter is that your life will be happier if your bank account is happier. Happy wife equals happy life, but happy bank account equals happy wife! I hear people talking about the importance of choosing a profession they enjoy. That sounds good but work is work and enjoying life means choosing a profession your bank account enjoys. If my profession was licking popsicles all day, after a while I'd get tired of living in poverty even though I was getting paid to lick popsicles!

Janet and I have two children—Carson and Rebecca. When they were nearing high school graduation, there were obligatory career choice discussions. We stressed the importance of choosing a productive career path instead of just a college major. Only 47 percent of college graduates find a job in the field of their major. I've heard of too many who earned a college degree in Canadian studies, comic art, or puppetology only to graduate with four years of debt and no *job-ology*. The number-one goal of a B.A. is a J.O.B. Graduating with a B.S. and no promise of a job is . . . you get the point.

Carson attended law school and Rebecca is a pharmacist. When Becca was an undergraduate student at Lipscomb University, she called one day to announce she was changing her major to band director. I'm going to offend all the band directors in the world, but Becca had been valedictorian of her high school class and we had higher hopes, for her sake. She had been an

All-Midstate trumpet player in high school and had fond memories of those days. This came under the heading of enjoyable profession versus enjoyable bank account profession.

We handled her very carefully and let the thought process take its course. She eventually made the right decision. I'm sure studying for those impossible biochemistry exams at midnight had challenged her ambitions. Becca never made a single "B" in one course from kindergarten through high school graduation. She's the consummate straight-A student and has continued that discipline to a very successful pharmacy career. She is also an outstanding Christian mother and wife. She's a pharmacist who's married to a pharmacist, so we don't have to go far to buy drugs.

Solomon wrote, "Train up a child in the way he should go and when he is old, he will not depart from it." I've heard pastors emphasize the last clause of the sentence implying the reason a child departed from faith is because they weren't trained right. The clergyman was trying to put parents on a guilt trip. The actual Hebrew emphasis is on the first clause. When you help a child find a profession that suits their personality and natural attributes, you're helping them find "the way they should go." It's your part in helping them discover the secret of success.

Definition of Wealth

I'm sure you noticed I used the term *wealth* for the third benchmark instead of financially stable or similar. *Wealth* is a relative term, and if you have $3,000 in the bank, you're in the top 50 percent of the wealthiest people in the world. If you have $70,000, you're in the top 10 percent; $1,000,000 equals top 1 percent. I suspect most people reading this book have $3,000 in the bank and many have $70,000. You're wealthy! The secret of success is not just keeping the wolf away from the door. Real success is reaching some measure of wealth. If you're happy living week to week or off the government, this book might not be for you.

Dave Ramsey uses the expression *everyday millionaire*. When what you own exceeds what you owe by $1M, you're an everyday millionaire. He allows adding up equity in your house, cars, and other assets along with bank savings to reach that total. It's not the same as having $1,000,000 in cash, but it's a morale booster. Everyone wants to be a millionaire!

In America, 9 percent of the population are everyday millionaires. That's the good news. The bad news is that a million bucks is no longer a million bucks. Inflation is the enemy of wealth, the crabgrass of bank accounts. Someone who retired twenty years ago with $1M felt fairly good about their retirement years, but not now. In just the past twelve months, the cost of housing has nearly doubled and abomination of abominations, a Big Mac meal costs $10! Wife to hubby, "Tonight we'll finally be in the black. We don't have enough money to pay the light bill!"

I might sound like an old man, but the future for American economics does not appear bright. No nation has survived long term by printing money to meet budgetary requirements. Can you imagine how much better your personal budget would work if you could just print new money each month to make ends meet. "Hey Honey, let's give the family down the street a new car this month. Maybe they'll like us better. We can just print money to pay for it!"

As mentioned earlier, our national debt has grown to $31 trillion at this writing, doubling in the past ten years. To pay it off, every American would need to ante up $100,000, but every taxpayer would shell out $250,000! Our nation spends $965M per day on debt interest alone! The only U.S. president who wiped out the entire national debt was Andrew Jackson in 1835. In the words of Dave Ramsey, we were "debt freeee!!" But that didn't last long as by 1837 we were debt *unfreeee* again. The debt increased from $65 million to $2.7 billion during the Civil War. By the end of World War I, our debt was $25B and after WWII $260B. The best day for a congressional session is the day of adjournment!

There are two ways to reduce federal debt—increase taxes or reduce federal spending. The latter doesn't seem very popular in D.C. A good start would be balancing the federal budget but politicians who try that are introduced to cancel culture. Increased interest rates, decreased savings, inflation, national security risk, reduced private investment, less income, and higher unemployment are results of federal debt. Raising the debt ceiling to solve our nation's problems makes about as much sense as raising the blood-alcohol levels to solve drunk driving. And which state in the union has the highest per-capita income? Maryland, of course, where many federal workers live. No wonder it's a swampy state!

To compound matters, America is the most taxed nation on the planet. Just in my little world, I'm liable for income, sales, property, capital gains, gas, hotel, firearms, payroll, estate, gift, Medicare, Social Security, building permit, air transportation, driver's license, hunting/fishing license, car license plate, Obamacare excise, and sports stadium tax. There are ninety-seven listed in the U.S. tax code (not counting state and local), and at this writing, the Biden administration just passed another large income tax increase and hired eighty-seven thousand new IRS agents to collect it. Their motto— "We have what it takes to take what you have."

I don't like to think about tax rates. If your annual income is $100,000, it's easy to see $50,000 going to someone else. Income (20-30%), sales (10%), property (.6%), capital gains (20%), hotel (7%), building permit ($.34 per sq ft), car gas ($.26 per gallon), Social Security (6.2%), Medicare (1.45%), and air transportation (7.5%) are just a few. Mark Twain said the only difference between a taxidermist and tax collector is the taxidermist only takes the skin.

At this writing I just turned sixty-five years old. I'm eligible for Social Security but will get a couple hundred bucks more each month by waiting eighteen months. Janet and I are still working and don't need the money now, so we've decided to wait. I'll need the extra to pay the income tax on my Social Security benefit! Are you kidding?? And according to the CBO, Social Security is set to run out of money in 2037. That's only fifteen years out. Apparently, the plan is to reduce monthly SSI payments by some 25 percent or more when that happens.

We've been paying Social Security tax (6.2%) on every dollar earned for more than fifty years. The government has taken hundreds of thousands of our dollars, not counting lost interest. If you average making $75,000 a year for fifty years, that equals $3,750,000 income. You were taxed 6.2% on that amount for a total of $232,500. And according to the Rule of 72, investments that earn an average of 7% annually double every ten years. Get the picture? The Great Society takes a great amount of your money. But the real tragedy is that your children and grandchildren will pay the tax and probably never receive a dime.

The New Good Ole' Days

So, there are many reasons to be pessimistic about the future of America, but there are also many reasons to be thankful. I hear people talking about the 'good ole days' referring to the fifties and sixties. I can tell you firsthand you're living in the good ole days in many ways!

When I was a boy in the sixties, very few families had a 3,000-square-foot house and most only one car. Now three or more autos are parked in the driveway because there's too much junk in the three-car garage of the

3,000-square-foot house! Thirty years ago, cars lasted only about 100,000 miles, but now they run longer with less repair. And minimum wage workers are making $15 an hour.

In just the last twenty-five years, new advances include the Internet, laptop computer, iPad, smartphone, Facebook, PayPal, Amazon, Door Dash, cable television, XM radio, HDTV, Wi-Fi, GPS, email, price scanner, fitness center, healthier food, Uber, fuel injector, smart thermostat, electric car, farm equipment with A/C, along with many medical and pharmaceutical advances. Millions around the world are healthier because of a new medical procedure or pill.

One of the hottest new investments is artificial intelligence (AI). Self-driving cars, personal assistants, automated investing, robotics, and nonintrusive healthcare are just a few uses for AI. Humans tend to make decisions irrationally, but machines are not affected by mood or extenuation.

When I was a child very few people could afford to fly internationally, but now it seems like everybody's been to Europe! We have high speed trains traveling 200 MPH, and three-star hotels are more luxurious than five-stars of yesteryear. Fifty years ago, eating out was a rare luxury for a few, but now it's a daily option for many. With my trusty cell phone, I can control my garage door and thermostat, buy stocks, order a pizza, identify plants, and take a photo . . . and get an answer to most every question via Google voice! *These are the good ole days.*

And yet, how do we afford it all? Cars do last a lot longer, but they also cost a lot longer. Pharmacist to patient, "The most common side effect of this medication is loss of disposable income." Bubba said he was so broke he couldn't even afford to pay attention.

Act Your Wage

There are three ways to have more money— less debt, less spending, and/or more income. The title of my next book is *The Secret of Money* which goes into detail about debt, spending, and income. The following paragraphs are general thoughts.

If you're a Dave Ramsey disciple, you know he's all about less debt. "Debt alters the course and condition of your life. You no longer run it; you are owned. We buy things we don't need with money we don't have to impress people we don't like. If broke people are making fun of your financial plan, you're on the right track. Act your wage." Amen, Dave.

The benefits of being debt-free include more expendable income, improved credit score, earlier retirement, less stress, more choices, better job options, lower blood pressure, and better marriage. Two of life's greatest blessings are pain-free and debt-free. Debt freedom is financial self-defense. An ancient proverb says it's better to go to bed hungry than wake up in debt.

The *best* way to be debt-free is by counting every dollar every day. Like calories, you lose debt when you learn what's causing it. I have dealt with people through health insurance applications who hadn't looked at their bank account balance in months. It was too frightening. They didn't want to know. Anyone who tells you money is the root of all evil either doesn't have any or doesn't know they don't have any. Personal financial ignorance is not bliss. It's better to get hurt by the truth than comforted with a lie.

I have an Excel expense spread sheet which I update every morning. It has a list of expense categories such as eating out, groceries, clothes, car repair, entertainment, home repair, auto gas, etc. I input each expense from the previous day into the appropriate category and keep an exact total of our expenses. I have a record of our detailed finances for the past twenty-five years. Little details make a big financial difference.

In a recent month I noted we spent $3,000 eating out. That's too much! Even though it included birthday celebrations with the family, trips to the diner needed a diet. We made a conscious effort to eat at home a little more. If I was not counting every dollar, I might not have known. It's easy to spend blindly and compulsively. And yet, a budget lets you know what you can't afford but doesn't keep you from buying it.

The average American has $5,500 debt on a credit card which have an average interest rate of 16.4 percent. Just unbelievable! No wonder Visa spends $100 million on annual advertising. If you paid that debt at $200 per month, you'd pay $1,445 interest over a three-year period. That changes a $5,500 debt to a $6,945 debt. When Janet and I got back from our Daytona Beach honeymoon, we were tempted to max out our credit cards, but there's not a worse way to start a marriage.

I'm a believer in credit cards but only those which pay points and when the statement balance is paid in full every month. I have an Amazon card that gives 5 percent back on every Amazon purchase, a Visa card that returns 2 percent on every purchase, and an American Airlines card that builds airline flight points. I count on credit card reimbursements of $300-400 each month from the previous month's purchases. That's an annual vacation!

Dave Ramsey has an excellent debt-reduction program if you're in a bad situation. He says, "Live like nobody else now so you can live like nobody else later. You can't get out of debt by living the same lifestyle that got you there." The only person who sticks closer than a brother is a creditor.

Discipline Gives Liberty

The *second* way to have more money is less spending. Warren Buffett, "Don't save what is left after spending, but spend what is left after saving." Rich people stay rich by living like they're broke. Broke people stay broke by living like they're rich. One lady said she has several zero-interest credit cards… she pretty much lost interest in them once they got maxed out.

The best way to spend less is to create a budget and stick with it. Just like setting a max calorie budget trims pounds, setting a max spending budget trims the statement balance. Discipline gives liberty to fiscal life. As Janet and I approach retirement, we have a budget we follow each month. We don't like having month left over at the end of the money.

Yes, one easy way to spend less is cutting back trips to the Greasy Spoon. Eating out is bad for your health and your money clip. I'm preaching to myself! Entertainment, clothing, hobbies, and vacations can all be clipped. Reconsider your thermostat, avoid unnecessary driving, buy generic at the grocery store, avoid big car payments, contract minimal cell phone and cable packages . . . and avoid grandchildren. If you catch frugal fever, it can be a generous germ. Confucius, "He who will not economize will eventually agonize." Wise spending is a righteous habit of the wealthy. If Jimmy Carter can shop at Dollar General, you can, too.

And yet, from the 'you may be too frugal' department, I read about a man who collected 400,000 cans to pay for his wedding. They brought $3,800. Another lived on Groupons for a year, and another in a cave twelve months to avoid a mortgage. Spending less is a righteous habit unless it ruins your habitat. Bubba said, "My friends keep insisting I'm too frugal, but I'm not buying it!"

Money Generates Interest

The *third* way to have more money is to make more money. Men (and women) are like bank accounts, the more money they have, the more interest they generate. My uncle Maurice famously said he'd rather be miserable rich than miserable poor. Having money makes sense and having sense makes money. Kevin O'Leary, a.k.a. Mr. Wonderful, "Money has no gray areas. You either make it or you lose it."

When you saw the title of this book, I'm sure the first thing which popped into your mind was a dollar sign. We tend to equate success mostly with making money. And for granted, this is not a book about being happy in poverty but being successful financially. The great cities in America have been built because somebody made money. The great hospitals and medical advances exist because somebody made money. The beautiful cathedrals and churches of the world stand because somebody made money.

I worshipped at Westminster Abbey in London one Sunday morning. Since William the Conqueror in 1066, all British coronations have occurred there. The beauty and detail of the structure is breathtaking. It's called Westminster because it's west of St. Paul's Cathedral, another staggering structure. Charles and Diana were married there. Those two incredible cathedrals exist only because somebody worked hard and made money. Several years ago, I worshipped with Robert Schuller at the beautiful Crystal Cathedral in Los Angeles. It's one of the most beautiful church buildings in America and a perfect picture of hard-working, generous Christians!

The Bible is full of examples of people the Lord blessed with a large amount of money. Abraham, Isaac, Job, Solomon, David, Joseph, Hezekiah, Josiah, Boaz, Zacchaeus, Matthew, Joseph of Arimathea, Lydia, Dorcas, Barnabas, and Philemon. "The blessings of the Lord bring wealth." (Proverbs 10) "All blessings will come to you if you obey the Lord." (Deuteronomy 28) "Abram was very rich in livestock, in silver, and in gold." (Genesis 13) David gave Solomon three thousand tons of gold for building the temple.

I like *The Message* translation of Deuteronomy 28:13: "God will make you the head, not the tail; you'll always be the top dog, never the bottom dog, as you obediently listen to and diligently keep the commands of God." Wealth is a blessing from the Lord. The only tragedy of wealth is when it's not complemented by the other three benchmarks of success.

The following are ten tips for making more money and then I'll give an example of someone who found the secret. These are practical suggestions I've learned from fifty years of enjoying the Lord's blessings.

Tip No. 1: Wealth equals work. There are no shortcuts. Those who outwork and outlearn outearn. Opportunity is missed by many because it's disguised as work. Hard work beats talent when talent doesn't work hard. Start before you're ready.

My first introduction to hard work was a morning newspaper route at age fourteen. Getting out of bed at 3 A.M. isn't much fun for an eighth grader, and the bicycle is a frigid ride on a winter morning. But it introduced me to real life and was an early morning wake-up call to do better someday. I've been working almost every day since—fifty-two years.

I had a job in college loading trucks for UPS from 11 P.M. – 3 A.M. The job was not only hard physical labor but also required memorizing 200 zip codes. Talk about taking the zip out of college life! That was in 1977 and I was making $15 an hour, but it was a tough gig. I was also pastoring a rural church on Sundays. Sleep depravity was my college minor.

But I learned early that few things feel better than the joy of achievement at the end of a hard day's work. Learn to crave it and you'll never have to worry about keeping the lights on. The joy of accomplishment is a win-win. You feel good about yourself and your wallet. A verse from *Larry's International Version*: "Spend most days mostly working for the most satisfaction in life." Happiness is in the doing, not just the possessing. Success is never an accident.

The man for whom Janet and I can attribute much of our financial success is Troy McQuagge. He's the founder and CEO of US Health Advisors. Under his excellent leadership, the company has been honored with a Stevie Award every year since 2012. They have been honored as Company of the Year four times, and since inception have provided fifteen million people with health insurance. The primary reason for the company's success is the hard work and brilliance of Mr. McQuagge. Wealth equals work.

Tip No. 2: Wealth equals uncertainty. To be wealthy you must learn a regular job with a certain income is security but often poverty. Living week to week is a way to live weaker and weaker. For several years Janet and I have worked for a commission-only insurance company—we only make money if we make a sale. There are insurance companies that pay a guaranteed salary and accept the uncertainty for you, but they also accept more of the income for you. And you must still make sales to keep your job. As we learned how to make commission-only sales and then received a couple of bonus checks, the uncertainty became more certain.

A doctor has a large income because he lives with the uncertainty of performing surgeries without making a deadly mistake. A farmer plants a thousand acres of corn but is at the mercy of uncertain Mother Nature. A local car dealer has all the trappings of success because he has learned to live with commission-only uncertainty. The irony of living with uncertainty is that mastering it makes wealth more certain. The irony of living with certainty is that as it masters you, wealth becomes more and more uncertain. Risk tolerance is like disease tolerance, both are enhanced by exposure. Wealth equals uncertainty, at least initially.

Tip No. 3: Wealth equals problem solving. Wealthy people are successful problem solvers. The person who is most promoted is the person who solves the most problems. Rick Warren: "Life is a series of problem-solving opportunities. The problems you face will either defeat or develop you depending on how you respond to them." The easiest way to escape a problem is to solve it.

Sam Walton revolutionized buy-and-exchange policies for American retail. He famously said, "There is only one boss; the customer." If the customer has a problem with their purchase, successful companies offer a refund or exchange. A large retail store has a dedicated customer service department whose only job is solving problems. Walton: "The customer can fire everybody in the company from the chairman on down, simply by spending their money somewhere else."

When I wake up each morning, the first thing that pops into my mind are the problems for the day. I try to focus on the solution because it gives me energy for the solving. Begin with the end in mind. Robert Schuller: "Problems are not stop signs but guidelines." It takes more energy to avoid a problem than solve it. The chief problem solver is the chief moneymaker!

Tip No. 4: Wealth equals tax awareness. We live in a land of much taxation founded to avoid taxation. As it turns out, taxation with representation ain't so hot either. Like 'the IRS' says, it's all the*irs*. Those last three letters sound like it and look like it! A key to building much wealth is avoiding much tax. I pay every dime for which I'm liable, but not one *mite* more!

The first federal income tax in America wasn't created until 1861 to pay for the Civil War but was repealed in 1872. Can you imagine the tension of forcing Southerners to pay a new tax for the war they lost! In 1894 an income tax was reinstated as 2% for income over $4,000 but overturned by the Supreme Court in 1895. The income tax law as we know it today was passed in 1913 with Form 1040 released in 1914. The income tax rate for the bottom bracket peaked at 22.2% in 1952 and for the top bracket at 94% in 1944-45 during World War II. Many sacrifices were made both at home and abroad for our freedom.

Here are some legal strategies to reduce your income tax (from usnews.com):

- Contribute to a retirement account.
- Open a health savings account.
- Start a side self-employment business.
- Write off business travel, even on vacation.
- Deduct half your self-employment taxes.
- Deduct an earned income credit.
- Deduct private mortgage insurance premiums.
- Make a charitable donation.
- Invest in qualified opportunity funds.

There are numerous others. I've learned one of the best ways to reduce income tax is to employ an accountant. Janet and I have been blessed by the excellent advice of Richard Biggs, CPA for forty years. The tax prep software programs are fine if you're in a lower income bracket, but an advisor can save you money otherwise. Yes, billionaires like Jeff Bezos and Elon Musk have years when they pay zero income tax because of a shrewd advisor. I'll always be an advocate of Mike Huckabee's fair tax plan that advocates a national sales tax in lieu of income tax. It levels the playing field and seems fairer. It would also save the need for 87,000 new IRS agents . . . along with the 80,000 existing!

And about that income tax on your Social Security benefit, the law says if you earn between $25,000-34,000 annually, you pay income tax on 50% of your SS benefit. If you earn more than $34,000, you pay income tax on 85% of your benefit. Most fall into that latter category. Only in America do we pay tax on tax! We pay a new income tax on previously taxed income to pay a new income tax. It taxes my mind to write that! Who voted for these people? Oxygen is about the only thing left that's free but don't tell lawmakers. Wealth equals tax awareness.

Tip No. 5: Wealth equals time. If you look closely at an overnight success, you'll realize it took a long time to achieve. The rich view wealth as the result of long-term growth; the poor want instant gratification. The best time to save money is when you have some. A windfall usually means a shopping spree when it should mean saving for a rainy day.

According to Wikipedia, Harlan Sanders's famous fried chicken recipe was rejected 1,009 times before being accepted. Not sure where they got that number, but he wasn't worth $1 million until age seventy-four when he sold Kentucky Fried Chicken to Jack Massey. Judge Judy's show was first aired when she was fifty-four and Ray Croc convinced the McDonald brothers to franchise the restaurant at age fifty-two. Wealth is not usually an overnight success.

Michael Jordan is an American hero and great example of perseverance. When he was a sophomore in high school, he was passed over for the varsity team, but because he didn't quit, he capped off his career as a McDonald's All-American. He said, "I've missed more than 9,000 shots in my career. I've lost almost 300 games. Twenty-six times I've been trusted to take the game-winning shot and missed. I've failed over and over and over in my life. And that is why I succeed." Great words from the G-O-A-T!

In 1899, Henry Ford founded the Detroit Automobile Company, but it failed in 1901 because of his inability to pay back a loan to the Dodge brothers. He convinced one of his partners to give him another shot but he failed again. In 1903, he tried one more time at age forty. Henry found a backer named Alexander Malcolmson who made a fortune in coal and lent him the money to found Ford Motor Company. His goal was to produce cars that were affordable for the average American family. By the mid-1920s, Henry Ford's net worth was $1.2 billion.

Success is not final; failure is not final; it's the courage to persevere that brings success. The greatest oak was once a little nut that held its ground. I have run several half-marathons and one full twenty-six-miler. The toughest part is not the physical but the mental. The body is willing, but the mind wants a detour to Krystal. Wealthy people make up their minds to live life as a marathon, not a sprint. Wealth equals time.

Tip No. 6:- Wealth equals money management. You either learn to manage money or the lack thereof will manage you. Saving is as important as making. Dave Ramsey says to save 15 percent of every paycheck. Most people are stuck between "I need to save money" and "You only live once." The quickest way to double money is not to fold it over and put it in your back pocket. If you watched the recent Elvis movie you know money management was not his forte`.

According to Warren Buffett, the greatest money-management principle in the world is compounding. Albert Einstein said compounding is the eighth wonder of the world. If you have $10,000 invested, add $100 per month, and average 7% interest annually for thirty years, the compounded amount will be $203,000. That scenario starting with $50,000 will be $528,000. More on investing later.

A finance company will not lend money for a mortgage that exceeds 28 percent of gross income. Thus, with an annual income of $100,000 you cannot exceed a monthly mortgage of $2,800. I'd sure hate to think I was managing that mortgage with that income. And who was the evil one who designed amortization schedules that seem to apply 99.99% of the first ten years' mortgage payments to interest only?

From Dave Ramsey, a good *after income tax* monthly money-management plan:

- Needs 50%
- Wants 30%
- Save 10%
- Tithe 10%

If you have a $100,000 annual income, income tax will be about $23,000 which leaves $77,000 to manage:

- Needs: $38,500 ($3,208 monthly)
- Wants: $23,100 ($1,925)
- Save: $7,700 ($641)
- Tithe: $7,700 ($641)

In that scenario, about $500 per week is left over for eating out, movies, vacations, ordering from Amazon, and other things. That requires a lot of discipline in our material world. One Saturday night family excursion to Chuck E Cheese and The Lion King is 25 percent of that $500. Most importantly—keep up with every dollar every month. And look for ways to make more than $100,000 per year!

Tip No. 7: Wealth equals preparation. One of my life's achievements is Eagle Scout. Robert Baden-Powell, the English soldier who began the Boy Scouts, published the motto "Be prepared" in his 1908 handbook. Scoutmaster Danny Goodpasture was one of the most uplifting influences of my upbringing. I remember him teaching me the motto as a thirteen-year-old boy in Troop 772. I've been reminded all through life that being prepared is a key to success. Zig Ziglar said success is found when opportunity meets preparation.

Abraham Lincoln, "If I had an hour to cut down a tree, I'd spend the first forty-five minutes sharpening the axe." Being prepared is vital for each day's success—a good night's sleep, a healthy breakfast, a planned agenda, a prepared mind, a positive attitude, a laugh, and if possible, a trip to the gym. And yes, I believe a morning cup of coffee is a wake-up hug for the brain. The thing that goes best with a hot cup is another hot cup.

Preparation for a profession is crucial. If you're in sales, become an expert in psychology; a homebuilder, knowledge of cutting-edge house plans; an accountant, familiar with the new tax laws. An attorney representing a client in court spends 90 percent of his time preparing for the presentation. Ben Franklin: "By failing to prepare you're preparing to fail."

One key to financial preparation is a good credit score. In today's online world, it's at the top of the checklist. Credit scores are an assessment of honesty and integrity. Check your score at AnnualCreditReport.com but not too often or it will go down. Equifax, TransUnion, and Experian are the credit reporting agencies. If you created a bad score over a ten-year period, it can't be repaired in a couple months. But the repair will be a down payment on your financial future. Preparation exponentiates wealth.

Tip No. 8: Wealth equals personal growth. Success is like a summer flower, either growing or dying. A lack of sunshine, nutrition, and water results in a wilted flower. A lack of mental, physical, social, and spiritual nutrition results in a wilted ambition. Personal growth is the shadow of preparation.

Many personal growth books are mostly fantasy, about as useful as a white crayon. They sound good on paper but have little practical value. The rhetoric is motivational for a brief time, but quickly fizzles. I've tried to write this book practically and personally, but how can you make it last? For me, learning about more personal growth for a sustained period has always boiled down to *when*. And the time slot I've stuck with is just before sleep. I keep a Kindle on my nightstand and read fifteen minutes each night in bed. It helps me unwind and offers an inspiring thought for morning application. I also read the Bible each year on my tablet, usually before getting out of bed in early morning. Personal growth is about sustained discipline. The bad news is time flies; the good news is you're the pilot.

Mark Cuban is owner of the NBA's Dallas Mavericks and star of *Shark Tank*. He was born in Pittsburgh, but at age twenty-four moved to Dallas, driving a Fiat with a hole in the floor. He tried bartending and failed; tried short-order cooking and failed; and was fired as a computer salesman. But he kept improving himself and eventually started a company called Micro-Solutions. He sold the company to CompuServe for $30 million at age thirty-two. He said, "I still work hard to know my business. I'm continuously looking for ways to improve all my companies, and I'm always selling. Always." Like Mark, make it a mission to fly a little higher each day!

It's easy to step back into safety but successful people step forward with personal growth. My life has an "Under Construction" sign perpetually posted because there is always something to improve. That sounds sexy and exciting, but real growth is messy and boring. And like Wi-Fi, when you unplug for a few minutes and reset, you're more powerful. Set goals and start plotting a pathway for their achievement. Self-improvement is a good addiction.

Tip No. 9: Wealth equals openness. Successful people are open to new ideas and opportunities. Someone said minds are like parachutes, they only work when they're open. Closed-minded individuals are more interested in being understood than understanding. They don't want their ideas challenged. Living life with an open mind will open many closed doors.

A useful feature of my Cadillac is a blind spot detector. When a car is in my blind spot, a little red light alerts me. Successful people realize they have a blind spot, and that a bad decision can be a deadly wreck. Looking back on my life, some of my worst experiences were working with a group of men who were living with a red light on. It worked their way fifty years ago and there was no reason to change. The result was a bad wreck. And in my experience, a closed mind usually means an open mouth.

Mary Kay Ash experienced divorce as a young lady and was forced to sell books door to door during World War II. She married again several years later and was in the process of starting a new business when her second husband died suddenly. She had an innovative *open* idea, however, and wasn't giving up. She wanted to open a 'cosmetics only' storefront in Dallas, something unheard of in the early sixties. Her oldest son loaned her $5,000 for the new venture. She said, "When God closes a door, He always opens a window." She died in 2001, but Mary Kay Cosmetics is still going strong with three million consultants achieving annual gross revenues of $3 billion.

Openness is an exciting, unexplored frontier. There is so much to learn and discover. To embrace the reality that you might be wrong is a sure sign you're exploring the right stuff. Curiosity is better than judgment. Our nation was founded on the principle of free speech and free dreams. Everyone has their say and their new idea. It's an open secret of making money.

Tip No. 10: Wealth equals teamwork. One ox can pull his own body weight, but two oxen yoked together can pull 10,000 pounds. Teamwork divides the task and multiplies the success. The strength of a team is each person; the strength of each person is a team.

The 80/20 rule is a reality of life—20% do 80% of the work, 20% give 80% of the money, and 20% are positive with 80% being negative. Companies that excel attempt to change those 20's to 100's. Sam Walton led a pep rally with his workers each Saturday morning to inspire teamwork. When "I" is replaced by "we" … illness becomes wellness.

One of the greatest victories of all-time was "Miracle on Ice." A team of amateur American hockey players defeated the professional Russian team in the 1980 Olympics. I remember watching it live. Mike Eruzione, the twenty-five-year-old US team captain, had given pep talks for months about teamwork. None of those boys went on to be dominant NHL players because their triumph was their teamwork.

The best teamwork for financial success is a happy marriage. The power of two people yoked together with love and grace is the economy's best friend. My wife is the ultimate team player. She's not very tall but has big shoulders. According to a recent survey, 86 percent of successful people have long-term marriages. Steven Curtis Chapman: "There's nothing like a good cheating song to make me want to run home to be with my wife." Doing battle with the world each day only to come home and do battle with your spouse each night is a recipe for a bad life. We're all better and happier together—soulmates working together as teammates. Wealth comes to offices where the golden rule is twenty-four carats.

Thus, there are three ways to have more money— less debt, less spending, and more income.

Secret Discovered

I promised an example of someone who discovered the secret. I know a man who was born into this world with a love for people. When he was six months old, his mom could hardly get through the grocery store because of his cooing at people from the infant seat. As a young boy, he was always leading a tribe of friends in the neighborhood. He was a natural leader. In high school, he was captain of his sports teams and voted most likely to succeed by his graduating class. When he got to college, he was elected president of his fraternity and eventually president of the student body.

He was accepted into law school and hated every minute. He spent three years studying in isolation. He was slowly dying without his people. After graduation, he had no desire to practice law and accepted a job with an insurance company. He was back with people. He made $2,000 in his first week. He was made for sales and willing to work eighty hours a week. At the end of his first year, he finished in the top ten with a company of ten thousand licensed agents.

He was promoted to manager. Now he was around even more people. His undergraduate major was management, so he had both natural skills and a college degree for this job. He was a natural at recruiting and motivating. His team began to grow. He was promoted to division manager. He rented space in a high-rise office building, signing contracts for which his law degree was useful. He recruited 125 agents over a three-year period and rented more space. At this writing, his annual income is $2 million at age thirty-five, and he did it all on his own.

I know this man fairly well because he's my son, Carson L. Rogers. He could be someone I've never met, and he'd still be a great example of someone who learned the secret of making money early in life. He has always made me look better than I deserve. I'm so proud of both my children.

Carson's wife, Lindsey Limerick Rogers, has also been successful in the insurance business and is descended from the great Packard family. Her great-great-grandfather, William Doud Packard, and his younger brother, James Ward, started Packard Electric Company in 1890. For ten years, they manufactured electric transformers, fuse boxes, measuring instruments, and cables. Then they became interested in a horseless carriage and bought a French De Dion-Bouton—a gas-powered tricycle. They believed they could build one themselves and negotiated the purchase of a gasoline engine from Charles King of Detroit. The rest is history.

Their first car was built in Warren, Ohio, on November 6, 1899. Operations were moved to Detroit in 1902. An Oldsmobile Runabout was selling for $650 at the turn of the twentieth century, but the Packard Roadster started at $2,600. It was a luxury automobile that appealed to the wealthy with the famous slogan: "Ask the man who owns one."

In 1915, they introduced the Twin-Six engine that was the first twelve-cylinder automobile in production. It was considered the greatest automobile innovation since the Mercedes Benz of 1901. That was the year the Germans produced the first car with an engine installed up front rather than under the seat. The automobile land speed record was set by a Packard in 1919 when the twelve-cylinder sped through the Daytona Beach dunes at 149 MPH. In 1928, gross income for the Packard company was $21 million. They sold twice as many cars abroad as other vehicles. William and James Packard are the embodiment of the ten tips for wealth and the American dream.

The term "American dream" was coined in the best-selling book, *Epic of America*, in 1931. James Truslow Adams described it as "that dream of a land in which life should be better and richer and fuller for everyone, with opportunity for each according to ability or achievement." It's a dream come true for the Packard brothers, Carson & Lindsey Rogers, and Drew & Rebecca Bracey. And it can be a reality for you!

Make Money While You Sleep

Warren Buffett: "If you don't find a way to make money while you're sleeping, you'll work until you die." He's talking about investing in the stock market.

The New York Stock Exchange traces its beginning to 1792 when merchants gathered casually in coffeehouses on Wall Street to trade stocks—a small ownership in a large company. The first transactions were handwritten on small sheets of paper. The New York Stock Exchange officially opened in 1817 when twenty-four merchants gathered under a Buttonwood tree to sign the Buttonwood Agreement.

This led to various stock market exchanges and ultimately a global market. The U.S. stock markets have averaged gains of 9% per year since 1900 despite two world wars, the Great Depression, the assassination of presidents, 2008 economic downturn, and Covid-19.

I had been dabbling in the market for several years before making my first stock market investment through a brokerage office in 1992. I invested $200,000 with a firm in downtown Nashville. We had just sold our house and moved to Kennett, Missouri, to work with a church and live in a parsonage. At the time, I thought I'd leave the money invested ten years, but we were quickly homesick. After a couple years, we moved back to Tennessee to work with another church, but no parsonage.

I needed money for a house down payment and you guessed it, my stock account was down 10 percent. I had to take capital from a depreciated principal which is never a good thing. If you can only remember one statement from this book about money and investing, remember this: *Entrusting your money to an individual stockbroker will make you broker*. Mutual funds are the biggest rip-off in the financial world. There are numerous hidden fees that eat up to 4% of the annual profit. If you're hoping for that magical 9% average annual return on your investment, you're paying over half of it to a broker and they get their cut regardless of how the markets perform. More details in my next book. Warren Buffet, "Wall Street is the only place that people ride to in a Rolls Royce to get advice from people who take the subway."

So, you ask, "How do I invest my money?" My advice is to open a personal account with an online broker (e.g., Fidelity, Charles Schwab, Ameritrade) and manage your money through index funds. They track the market indexes (Dow Jones, Nasdaq, S&P, etc.) without the large broker fees. The index fund fees are much less (usually less than 1 percent) and some funds have zero fees. An index tracks a composite or group of companies, such as those listed with the S&P 500. Your money is safer when its value is based on the performance of 500 or more companies. Since 1817, the indexes have always eventually returned to their all-time high and beyond. That is not necessarily the case with the individual companies that make up a traditional mutual fund, and every time your broker advises you to buy or sell a stock within that fund, he gets a commission for which you pay a fee!

Examples of safe index funds include DIA that tracks the Dow Jones Index, QQQ tracks the Nasdaq, and SPDR the S&P 500. If you simply invested your money in those three funds and left it for thirty years, your money would triple if the markets followed historic trends. Online brokerage firms employ advisors who will guide you through the step-by-step process free of charge. If you're uncertain about managing your own money, get your feet wet by starting with a small amount. Open an online account and transfer $3,000. Invest $1,000 in each fund—DIA, QQQ, and SPDR. Don't buy when the indexes are at an all-time high but wait for a slight correction. Learn the ropes for a year or so and compare your results to mutual funds.

The fact that you're reading this book indicates you might read another. While on vacation several years ago, I stumbled into a mall bookstore and picked up a small book that changed my financial life. *The 3% Signal* by Jason Kelly is the most practical investing book I've read. I could not recommend it highly enough! It will open your eyes to index fund investing and close your interest in brokers and mutual funds!

If you're interested in having a little more hands-on approach to stock market investing, there are three general approaches. Here's a brief synopsis of each:

- **Buy and hold.** This method is to buy stock in a company or index fund and leave it invested indefinitely. Nobody has made more money investing than Warren Buffett. He's famous for the quote, "If you can't afford to hold a stock 10 years, don't even think about owning it 10 minutes." His net worth is $100 billion so it's hard to argue with his logic.

- **Swing trading.** This investing style is to buy a stock and hold it for a few days or weeks. Maybe the markets will have a slight correction on a day and the price of a hot stock goes down. The fundamentals of the economy seem good, and you believe the price decrease was just a bad day. You buy shares at a low price with the intention of selling them when the price *swings* back up in a few days or weeks. The markets often swing in increments of three days. My primary mode for swing trading is options. More in the next book.

- **Day trading.** This is a method of completing the transaction of buying and selling stocks during the same day, sometimes completing a trade in minutes or seconds. In today's online world, there are numerous computer graph indicators that give real time short-term buy and sell signals. All transactions are completed on the same day with a zero-account balance at the market's close. An excellent book for this type of trading is *How to Day Trade for a Living* by Andrew Aziz.

I use all three methods in my portfolio. I have 85 percent invested for the long term in safe ETF index funds, swing trade with 10 percent and day trade with the remaining 5 percent. Since I work from home, I have time to watch the markets and trade throughout the day. It's hard to imagine ever trading stocks without the Internet.

One of the biggest factors for stock market investing is tax liability. When a capital asset is sold for more than its original purchase price it results in a capital gain. Capital assets include things like stocks, bonds, precious metals, and real estate. The amount of tax paid depends on how long the asset is held.

A long-term capital gain is generally an asset held for more than one year. The tax rate for that gain can range from 0-20% but is generally less than a short-term capital gain that's taxed based on your income tax bracket for the current year. Short-term tax rates generally range from 10-37%.

As you can see, buying and holding a stock usually incurs less tax liability than swing or day trading. If you're not yet seventy-two years old, however, one way to defer tax liability is to trade in your IRA, 401(K), or other retirement account. You are not taxed on that income until you're forced to withdraw a minimum required amount at age seventy-two. Theoretically, your income tax rate will be less at that age. I swing trade with options mostly in my IRA account. More on that in my next book.

The best way to learn about stock market investing is clicking the mouse. Experience is the best teacher. When the Iraq War started in 2001, one of the highest-rated stocks was a company that made armored vehicles and weapons for war. It seemed like a no-brainer. *Investor's Business Daily* listed it at the very top of their list. I jumped in with $5,000. The price went down a little, so I bought another $5,000 at a bargain. A couple weeks later another $5,000 at a "better bargain."

As it turned out, the company seemed like a good idea but was poorly managed. I ended up losing all my money! It's the only stock for which that happened in forty years of trading. I learned from the experience to do better homework and put most of my money in index funds instead of individual stocks. Warren Buffett, "The know-nothings can outperform the professionals by investing in index funds."

Algorithms Function Better than the Government

Last year I decided to join the crowd and buy a small amount of cryptocurrency. I averaged-in $5,000 over a three-month period. The first decentralized crypto was called Bitcoin, released in 2009 by Satoshi Nakamoto. That person or group is unknown as their identity has never been confirmed. Very unusual situation! Nakamoto is the name of the person who wrote a paper about cryptocurrency in 2008 and is thought to have been the originator, but he says, "Not me!" The first financial transaction was the purchase of two Papa John pizzas for 10,000 Bitcoins in 2009. Although cryptocurrency has lost nearly half its value in the past year, the value of those 10,000 Bitcoins today is an astounding $200 million.

The idea is to provide an online, digital currency that operates independently of a centralized bank. Cryptocurrency is a complicated mathematical equation which includes new financial terms like blockchain, altcoin, fiat, gas, mining, non-fungible token, and others. When Russia invaded Ukraine, some Ukrainians feared that Russia would gain control of their banks and money, so they invested their money in cryptocurrency. The same thing happened in Venezuela. Unfortunately, their money has lost some of its value in the past year due to worldwide inflation and hacker theft, but it will likely come back. I do not have plans to purchase any more bitcoins, but also do not plan to sell my coins. I'm going to be a buy-n-hold bitcoin *Buffetologist*!

Working at Living

Somebody said retirement is the time when you stop lying about your age and start lying around the house. And what do you call a person who's happy on Monday morning? Retired! The only requirement for a happy retirement on Monday morning is lying around with financial peace the other days of the week. It's more fun to jiggle the fishing line when you have a happy bottom line.

The question is often not what age, but what income you choose to retire. According to Vanguard, the U.S. average total savings at retirement is $142,000. Since some have a lot more, many have a lot less. According to the U.S. Census Bureau, 35 percent of retirees have zero savings. The challenge for them is spending time without spending money.

According to Dave Ramsey, if you want an annual income of $50,000 during retirement, you'll need a nest egg of $625,000; for an income of $100,000, you'll need $1,300,000. He's including both investment and Social Security income in those totals. Unfortunately, the past year's inflationary concerns have made both less valuable.

From Nerd Wallet, you'll need to replace 80% of pre-retirement income for a happy retirement. Fidelity Investments' guidelines for retirement are to save 1X your income by age 30, 3X by 40, 6X by 50, 8X by 60, and 10X by 70. Thus, if your annual household income is $150,000 when you retire at age seventy, you'll need a nest egg of $1,500,000 to maintain your current standard of living.

How much retirement savings can you spend? Most experts suggest 3-4% annually. If you have $1,000,000 invested, you can take $30,000-40,000 per year; $1,500,000 would pay you $45,000-60,000. That's in addition to

Social Security income. In a perfect world your investments will gain 7-10% annually so your principal will hold its own.

The financial challenge for retirement is not the regular expenses, but the unexpected. Car repair, new roof, leaky dishwasher, root canal, and/or a year-end special offering at church are not in the budget. Your best plan will have a line item for the expected as well as the incidental. 'Underestimate and overcompensate' is a good rule for level living.

If you invest $1,500,000 in an immediate annuity, you'll have a guaranteed income of $91,500 per month for life. That might sound good, but when you die the remaining annuity cash goes to the insurance company.

The happiest people in retirement are those who retire from work but not from life. Retirement is not the end of the road, but the beginning of a new highway. The acrostic of R-E-T-I-R-E is Relax-Entertain-Travel-Indulge-Remember-Enjoy. Most have worked hard six to seven days a week for fifty years: it's time for a little RETIRE. Just when the caterpillar thought his life was over, he began to fly.

Best Insurance Is Insurance

Peace of mind at any age is spelled I-N-S-U-R-A-N-C-E. Modern insurance traces its origins to the Great Fire of London in 1666 when thirty thousand homes were destroyed. Nicholas Barbon started a homeowner's fire protection insurance company ten years later. Lloyds of London was founded in 1688. Ben Franklin created the first insurance company in America in 1752, modeled after the London firms.

"Buy all the insurance you can get your hands on" was advice from a wise man many years ago. Life, health, auto, homeowners, critical and long-term care protection should be part of your portfolio. Having worked in the insurance business for many years, I can tell you it's a lot cheaper to buy it five years too early than one minute too late. My brother, David Rogers, is a bankruptcy attorney. A primary reason people declare personal bankruptcy is unpaid medical bills, a.k.a. not having enough health insurance.

A lack of adequate coverage is rarely due to lack of funds but lack of priority. I've visited people who were driving a BMW with a $500 monthly car payment but had no health insurance. They were watching a big-screen TV, eating out, and enjoying every Walmart toy, but "couldn't afford" health insurance. They were hoping the government would bail them out. One of the first steps toward success is making priorities a priority.

I knew a man who needed and received a liver transplant but had no health insurance. He was fortunate to find doctors who were rich in mercy. I knew another man who died young and left behind three precious young daughters, but no life insurance. Being protected is more about the financial well-being of your family than yourself. If you have insurance on your cell phone but not your life, you might need to reevaluate your cells.

My father-in-law owned a successful trucking business that spread fertilizer and lime on local farmland. He also raised Charolais beef cattle on his farm in Bon Aqua, Tennessee. And yes, the area is as beautiful as the name. He worked eight days a week most of his life and saved a considerable sum of money. He did not believe in the value of health insurance, however, and his wife was diagnosed with cancer. It was a long, protracted battle and eventually took her life at age fifty-eight. They were honorable and paid every dime they owed the doctors and hospitals. It took a lot of their savings. We can make ten thousand good decisions in life, but one bad can do a lot of damage.

Don't fall for the Medi-Share trap. It sounds good in ads, and you might save a couple hundred bucks on monthly premium, but the coverage doesn't have maximum out-of-pocket protection. It's technically not insurance. If you get cancer and have a $500,000 bill, you could get stuck with half of it. With actual health insurance, after you reach a max-out-of-pocket of $5,000-10,000 (depending on policy), the insurance company usually pays 100%. Some Medi-Share policies don't cover surgical procedures and some doctors don't accept it. Make sure you read the policy very carefully and check with your doctor before choosing that option.

My mother's family has a history of spending time in a nursing facility, so she purchased long-term care insurance several years ago. To qualify for collecting the benefits, a patient must be unable to perform two of the six activities of daily living—bathing, eating, dressing, toileting, transferring, and continence. She is struggling with a couple of those at this writing and recently toured assisted-living facilities. She learned they are expensive, in the ballpark of $8,000-$12,000 per month, but her long-term care will pay $150 a day or $4500 a month. That payout along with her Social Security check will foot a lot of the bill. Buy all the insurance you can get your hands on!

Dave Ramsey recommends coverage for life, auto, homeowners/renters, health, long-term disability, long-term care, identity theft, and umbrella (coverage beyond existing limits) insurance. He must have talked to the same wise man as me! Dave's not a big fan of whole life insurance and neither am I. Life insurance is made for protecting life, not producing investment returns. Put your hard-earned money in twenty-year term life insurance and index funds for better results.

Dental insurance is a waste of money. I've gotten calls through the years from people saying, "I want to buy your best dental insurance policy *today!*" What they meant was, "I want to pay a $50 premium and get a $2,500 crown *tomorrow*." No company can stay afloat like that so dental insurance has a pre-existing clause. Most stipulate you have the insurance eighteen months before they will pay for surgical procedures and then there are scheduled limits—the policy specifies how much they'll pay per procedure.

Most dental policies do offer free cleanings but those are inexpensive, and dentists give a discount for cash. Only three months' premiums would cover the cleaning. I'm convinced cleanings are a smoke screen for recommending a $2,500 crown! Dentists charge too much and need more regulation. But yes, when you have a toothache, it doesn't matter. Just writing this paragraph makes me want to floss.

I read an article recently about how wealth and mental health are linked. Not only do finances affect your ability to afford insurance, but the impoverished are five times more likely to have poorer mental health. Those who earn $100,000 reported five times fewer 'incidents of sadness' than those making under $35,000. And having the cash to replace that missing front incisor is a big boost for self-esteem. Like red blood cells flowing through the entire body, finances affect the whole person.

Complements of the Third Mark

One of the most memorable days of my Hickman County childhood was an armed bank robbery. About 10:00 one Wednesday morning, three masked men burst into the First National Bank lobby with a sawed-off shotgun, rifle, and pistol. They ordered the clerks into the bank safe to get money. The tellers came out with $125,000! That was a lot of money in 1974. The robbers sped off in a van, ditched the weapons, and hid the stash in a barn. According to a newspaper report, the heist was the largest in Midstate memory.

A few minutes later, everybody in the county was on the public square speculating about the burglary. It was like a scene out of the Wild West. Who did it? How much did they get? Which direction did they go? Who wants to form a posse? As it turned out, the 'robber boys' were well-known locals who had gotten high and done something stupid. One of them was the son of the county trustee who was working in the courthouse across the street from the bank. And irony of ironies, the foolish boys came back to the public square after stashing the cash to mingle with the crowd asking, "Who dunnit??"

Just fourteen hours later, Sheriff Frank Atkinson had it all figured out and they were in jail. All but $196 of the stash was recovered. They paid a big prison price for that foolish heist. Money causes crazy notions! Work hard, save hard, invest hard, and you won't have to think hard about robbing a bank.

A few fun facts to close the chapter—it costs more to make a penny and a nickel than they're worth. It costs 2.1 cents to make a penny and 8.52 cents for a nickel. Nickels are not made of nickel but a combination of manganese, copper, and silver. A quarter has 119 edge grooves. The grooves are there because folks shaved the edges when the coins were pure metals. Paper money is not paper but 25% linen and 75% cotton. There are 293 ways to make change for a dollar. The Secret Service was initially created to stop counterfeiting. Warren Buffett's net worth at age fifty-two was just 0.3% of his current worth at age ninety-two (now over $100 billion). If any of those come up in trivial pursuit, you're ready!

So, Janet and I survived that first winter in Antarctica, a.k.a. the cold duplex. By spring we were still broke but excited about building a life together. She was working for an accounting firm and would soon move to a law firm and be promoted to paralegal. I owned a small landscape design business. It wasn't too glamorous, but I managed a six-figure income by the second year. I remember when we finally saved $25,000 after a couple of years. We thought we were set for life! We went out and bought a house, of course! Today, we look back on those days as some of our most treasured.

Try to enjoy the journey. Set goals and celebrate their accomplishment. Don't wait for everything to be perfect before loving your life. Stop occasionally and take advantage of the view. The mirage will become a destination soon enough and life's potholes will be a distant memory. Live life proactively and optimistically. Be positive when others are negative. Don't follow the crowd. Cherish every dawn of every new day of your sacred life. It's your one and only.

"How joyful are those who fear the Lord and delight in obeying his commands. Their children will be successful everywhere; an entire generation of godly people will be blessed. They themselves will be *wealthy*, and their good deeds will last forever." (Psalms 112)

The third leg of the bench is *wealth*. Life will never sit very comfortably until that mark fits securely. Eccentric Howard got this one right!

"I want my children to have all the things I couldn't afford, then move in with them."
— Phyllis Diller

4

THE SPIRITUAL

Y OU HAVE LEARNED ABOUT THREE BENCHMARKS FOR TRUE SUCCESS—physical health, social vitality, and abundant wealth. They thrive as adjuncts,
supporting and enhancing each other. You might have a zillion bucks but
abuse your body with a zillion bites and ruin your zest for life. You might be
the best specimen at CrossFit but have no special friends and miss out on
total fitness. Equal parts are needed to shape a whole person. Now we come
to the final mark for the bench— spiritual health. It completes and empowers
a successful life.

I was born into this world as a small-town preacher's kid. My life was
church, and church was my life. Our house was next door to the church
building. My brother and I played football and hide 'n seek in the sanctuary,
swam in the baptistry, and played horrible pranks on the janitor. You know
what they say about preacher's kids. The *spiritual* benchmark was chiseled
into my life at a young age.

Pierre Chardin is correct: "You are not a human being having a spiritual
experience. You are a spiritual being having a human experience." C. S.
Lewis: "You don't have a soul; you are a soul; you have a body." Rather than
just being aware of your thoughts and emotions, you realize there is an
awareness behind them.

Yes, we battle with the inner struggle to avoid one more donut; yes, we
battle with the inner struggle to forgive a co-worker and keep a friend; and

yes, we battle with the inner struggle to plunge into uncertainty, but our greatest inner battles are in the spiritual realm. "Our battle is not against flesh and blood, but against the spiritual forces of evil in the heavenly realm." (Ephesians 5)

Just as there are unseen radio waves oscillating throughout the atmosphere, there is an unseen spiritual world where a great battle is raging. Just as invisible Wi-Fi operates your laptop at 25 Mbps, there are invisible spirits controlling your daily life with many more megabits. "We fix our eyes not on what is seen but what is unseen, since what is seen is temporary but what is unseen is eternal." (2 Corinthians 4) But exactly how do the spirits work in that spiritual world? Where is it? What is it? How do you deal with it?

Foggy by Design

I've been doing battle in the spiritual realm for fifty-five years, trying to make sense of it. The existence of eternity is an incomprehensible concept for my brain. I cannot get my mind around the idea of a God out there with no beginning and no end. It makes me uneasy and frightened. It is unsolved mental territory and hostile to my conceivability. My brain is 60 percent fat, not fully formed until age twenty-five, and transfers messages at 268 MPH, but it is incapable of computing time without beginning or end.

And how did He create something out of nothing? Things in my little world are mostly determinate. I know the month my car was manufactured, the day my toy poodle was born, and the year my house was created. And I know they will eventually cease to exist. They have a beginning and an ending.

And yet, my spirit is eternal. It had a beginning at conception but will have no end. My body will return to the dust from which it was made, but my spirit will return to the Lord from which it was made.

What exactly is my spirit? It's my unseen inner person which interacts with that unseen spiritual realm. My prayers are offered through my spirit, and I worship through my spirit. "God is spirit and those that worship Him must worship in spirit and truth." (John 4) My spirit allows me to contact and receive God. Billy Graham: "The Holy Spirit is the One who makes you born again." "He (Jesus) breathed on them, and they [disciples] received the Holy Spirit." (John 20)

I have two spiritual natures at battle in my spirit—fallen and born-again. This mini-battle is indicative of the larger war raging in the vast, unseen spiritual realm. Star Wars is more fact than fiction. The forces of Satan are battling the forces of the Savior. My fallen nature is a result of Adam's fall in the Garden of Eden, which brought the curse of sin. My born-again nature is a result of Jesus's resurrection from that garden tomb, which erased the curse of sin. The extent to which I surrender my born-again nature to the control of Jesus through the indwelt Holy Spirit is the extent to which I have victory over my fallen nature, controlled by Satan. The process seems mysterious and obscure, but like connecting your cell phone to the 'unseen' Bluetooth earbud wave, our Creator has designed a very simple plan for connecting to success. Keep reading.

What is my soul? How is it different from my spirit? The soul is the mind, character, emotions, and will that function at the center of my thought. The Greek word for *soul* is *psyche* or the totality of conscious and unconscious awareness. The soul mediates responses between my born-again and fallen natures. A coach psyches-up his team before a game, motivating the entire person or *soul*.

Mary, the mother of Jesus, said, "My *soul* glorifies the Lord, and my *spirit* rejoices in God my Savior." There is clearly a difference between soul and spirit. Glorifying the Lord is a human or soul decision. Receiving God and rejoicing in Him (worship) is spiritual. Through my soul I evaluate myself and deal with my emotions, but through my spirit I evaluate God and deal with His emotions. *Soul* is synonymous with words such as *thoughts, imagination, desires,* and *emotions*. *Spirit* is synonymous with words such as *faith, prayer, hope,* and *praise.* Remember it like this—soul is more about self; spirit is more about Spirit. The spirit feeds the soul; the soul navigates the spirit.

Just as the triune God breathed life into Adam at creation, He breathed spiritual life into your soul at conception. "The LORD God formed man of dust from the ground and breathed into his nostrils the breath of life" (Gen 2). "The breath of God is in my nostrils." (Job 27) "The breath of the Almighty gives understanding." (Job 32) The Hebrew word for *spirit* is *ruach*, which means *breath* or *wind*. His eternal Spirit has been breathed into your temporal body—the very breath of God is sustaining you. It is no accident that breath is the source of both physical life and spiritual life.

The difference is that your spiritual breath is eternal. When your physical body is no longer breathing, your 'breathed spirit' will live on. It will live eternally either with the One who gave it breath or be eternally separated. "The spirit returns to the God who gave it." (Eccl 12). Jesus: "I give them eternal life and they shall never perish." (John 10) "Some will pay the penalty of eternal destruction; away from the presence of the Lord." (2 Thessalonians 1).

What is spiritual breathing? You exhale spiritually by confessing sins through prayer. You inhale spiritually by accepting the indwelling of the Holy Spirit to protect, empower, and forgive you. According to Bill Bright, "We exhale the impure and inhale the pure." One difference between physical and spiritual breathing is that physical is involuntary while spiritual is voluntary. We have free will. You can choose when you want to exhale sin and inhale the Spirit. Practice makes perfect.

When Peter, James and John were on the Mount of Transfiguration, Moses and Elijah appeared to them with a bright light. Even though Moses's body had been dead for fifteen hundred years, his spirit was still shining brightly. Elijah was one of two people mentioned in the Bible who never died. God took him to Heaven in a whirlwind, but when he left this earth, he began his spiritual existence. He was still going strong nine hundred years later. Just as the sun shines brightest when the atmosphere is cleared by rain, our spirits have their most brilliant radiance when the shroud of death is removed.

The brain never sleeps. From the moment you're born into this world, it is awake and responsible for bodily function. Your body sleeps, but the brain continues to work. In the same way, your spirit never sleeps and never dies. The sleepless Holy Spirit often speaks to our spirit through dreams. Joseph was told in a dream that Mary would be his wife. "He who watches over you will neither slumber nor sleep." (Psalm 121).

An Unconditional Condition

So, exactly how do you deal with your soul and spirit? How do you make sense of the realms, natures, and breath? I have learned there are two crucial words for living and thriving in the spiritual realm.

The first is *faith*. That might seem obvious and elementary, but it is an integral and absolute component of spiritual interaction. It must be fully understood that you were created by your Maker to be a creature of faith. The foundation for any discussion about spiritual realm interaction is not the Bible, baptism, prayer, obedience, heart-acceptance, or other theological checkmark. Those are ultimately important, but the foundation is unconditional faith.

How do you make sense of an eternal God? How do you understand 'something out of nothing?' How do you explain a leaf miraculously budding from a dormant tree branch? The birth of a child from living in a sack of water to breathing oxygen? The only answer is faith. If you're looking for everything in your life to be tangible and proven, you'll miss the secret of success. And if you think absolute proof is foolproof, the people who walked through the parted Red Sea and saw the sun stand still, quickly waned in their belief.

Faith is the number-one word in God's vocabulary and always the starting point. Martin Luther: "We are saved by faith alone, but the faith that saves is never alone." Martin Luther King, Jr.: "Faith is taking the first step even when you can't see the whole staircase." Just like a fish is created to live in water and a bird to fly in air, you are hard-wired to live by faith. God made you with two eyes, a nose, a mouth, and a relationship with Him through faith. It is his way of doing things and it's all encompassing!

You drive your car on a two-lane highway because you believe by faith the oncoming car will stay on their side. A farmer plants corn because he believes by faith clouds will produce rain. You expect the sun will rise in the East tomorrow morning by faith. Part of the reason you believe those things is because you've seen verifiable results in the past. But the same is true with spiritual faith. The results are verifiable. More on that in a few paragraphs.

I'm blessed to be born into a family of faith. The Rogers clan is not known for wealth like the Rockefellers or Vanderbilts, but as being rich in faith. Anyone in Centerville, Tennessee, who hears the words "Paul Rogers family" associates it with faith. My uncle Maurice Rogers traced John Rogers's lineage from England in the 1600s to Jamestown, Virginia, to North Carolina to Tennessee to Alabama. He discovered that a common denominator for our pedigree is faith. My mother can trace several generations of Restoration Movement Christians on her family tree. Her grandmother was friends with the great A. M. Burton who built the L&C Tower in downtown Nashville and kept Lipscomb University afloat during the Great Depression. He was a Christian who served as a church elder and is also the grandfather of singer Amy Grant. I've inherited a faith legacy and want to pass it on to my grandchildren and all God's children.

Noah had no tangible reason to believe God would flood the earth. His work was based entirely on faith. He built an ark for 120 years in a desert where it had apparently never rained. And Abraham is the 'father of the faithful' because he believed he could kill his 'one and only' son and God would bring him back to life. Sound familiar? The story of faith in Jesus is the theme of the entire Bible. You will always be frustrated with your spiritual life if you fail to underscore the preeminence of faith.

When I was a young boy learning to play golf, Dad taught me the interlocking grip. I wanted to grip the club with a baseball grip. It felt more natural. But I remember him saying, "If it feels wrong, it's right. Eventually it will feel natural and right." That has been my lifelong experience with faith. At first, it felt awkward and opalescent, but as years have gone by the fog has lifted and I can see clearly.

God's way is to test your faith and increase it when you trust Him through trials. George Mueller said those are the "food of faith." When that pet temptation pops into your mind and you resist, expect a blessing. And the Bible says God will provide a way of escape.

Every hero of the Bible interacted with Yahweh through faith. Read Hebrews 11. They tasted the food and trusted the Chef. Those who place all things in God's hands by faith will eventually see God's hand in all things by sight.

Hindsight Is 20/20

The second crucial word is *awareness*. My successful interaction in the spiritual realm depends on proactive awareness. When I was a boy, transistor radios became popular. It was fascinating to turn on the switch and connect to a radio wave. I remember being amazed I could listen to WLS some four hundred miles from Chicago. But it would only work if the antenna was pulled up. Otherwise, there was static.

I've learned that my interaction in the spiritual realm only works when my spiritual antenna is up, when I'm looking for a spiritual wave. God communicates with you through His Word, other people, an inner knowing, cleared and blocked paths, dreams and visions, intuition, and audibly. *That's one of the most important sentences in this book!* Remember the following words as you're starting your spiritual faith and awareness journey— 'Hindsight is 20/20.' Those are key to verification.

Weather prediction has improved dramatically in my lifetime. Meteorologists give a ten-day forecast that's remarkably accurate. Computers receive weather conditions from across the country and process the data for a forecast. The computers are programmed to remember how current weather conditions operated in the past and predict how they'll act in the future. When your awareness of God's past working in your life is programmed accurately, you can forecast the future outcome with remarkable accuracy.

A faith-building exercise is a prayer journal. Write down every prayer request every day. Write down specific goals, visions, and hopes for the future. Send them to the Lord in prayer and check off those that are answered. It is also spiritually awakening to keep a dream journal by your bed. My current pastor, Dr. Benjamin Pate, wrote his PhD thesis on how God communicates with us through dreams. It's one of the most exciting modes the Lord uses. Those journals will help you realize God is faithful, responsive, and verifiable. Hindsight is 20/20. More on prayer later.

I occasionally have a spiritual realization experience and feel something like a shiver come over my body (soul). For years I've read about Christians having Holy Spirit experiences and thought it to be foolishness, but it seems very real in recent years. I was at choir practice recently. We closed the session with a song that reminded me of something specific for which I'd prayed. As it occurred to me the Holy Spirit had obviously answered my prayer, I felt something like a shiver flush my body. You're thinking . . . this guy seemed fairly credible in those first three chapters, but now I'm not so sure. I can tell you that after walking closely with the Lord for fifty years, my interactions with Him are just as real to me as my interactions with my wife or children. The apostle Paul wrote, "The unbeliever does not receive the things of the Spirit of God, for they are foolishness to him. And he cannot understand them because they are spiritually discerned." (1 Cor 2) Max Lucado: "An orchestra leader must turn his back to the crowd."

Several years ago, Janet and I were both awakened in the middle of night by the same dream. We dreamed we were back in ministry, fulfilling our calling again. At that time, we had been out of ministry for ten years. We dreamed we were in the same building with the same people. When we compared notes, we were astounded by the identical details.

We believed the Lord spoke to us and we began looking for a church to serve. It wasn't long before a church door opened providentially. We were able to sell our house quickly in a tough market and everything fell into place. I believe the Lord spoke to us that night just as much as I believe I'm sitting in a chair writing about it.

When we decided to re-enter ministry, one of Janet's friends, Jean Blackwell, suggested they meet and pray. Jean is a faith-filled person who strongly believes in the indwelling power of the Holy Spirit. When she prayed, Janet said they clearly felt the presence of the Holy Spirit in the car. It was unlike anything she'd experienced.

I have much respect for Allen Jackson, pastor of World Outreach Church in Murfreesboro. It's one of the largest in Tennessee with some twenty thousand members. Janet and I have attended off and on for several years. I remember him talking about the Lord speaking to him audibly. He was in his car praying and initially thought his brother was playing tricks on him from the backseat, but realized his brother was nowhere around. As your spiritual awareness increases, the perceptiveness of your soul increases.

David Young has been the outstanding preacher for North Boulevard Church of Christ nearly forty years. It is one of the largest of their denomination with some three thousand members and multiple campuses. He was recently diagnosed with serious cancer, but during a hospital stay was awakened in the night by two angels standing at the foot of his bed. They told him he would be receiving healing and then disappeared. Thus far, that has been the case. I don't doubt David or believe it was a hallucination.

Janet and I planted a church in Columbia, Tennessee, in 2001 which brought us much persecution. It was a more progressive, open-minded church in a very conservative community. Several months after the church began, I was walking on a street near my house on a sunny afternoon. I've never experienced a time before or since when God spoke to me so clearly, but I remember being prompted to stop, look up, and listen. The Lord said two words that were as clear as a bell, "It's over." It was clearly an out-of-body experience. The words weren't audible, but I clearly heard them in my soul. It wouldn't be long before we left that church.

I hear Christians say things like, "I can't believe I was accepted into that college or got that job. It makes no sense. It seems like a miracle. There were a lot of people more qualified." Get your antenna up! Just like God performs a miracle on the tree branch in early spring, he's at work in the lives of His children. Much more so! Just like God performs a miracle when a baby is formed by the union of sperm and egg, he is active in daily stuff of your life. It's easier to believe God is involved than to believe coincidence. Faith is more predictable than chance. Singer and comedian Mark Lowry: "God spreads grace like a four-year-old spreads peanut butter. He gets it all over everything."

Innateness enhances awareness. Just as a calf is born with an instinct to suckle milk from his mother's utter, we are born with an innate instinct to discern some degree of right and wrong. In Romans 2, Paul was asked by gentile Romans about the eternal fate of their ancestors. The Old Testament says salvation was reserved only for Jews for several centuries. What about the Chinese who were living then? Mongolians? American Indians? What would be their eternal fate? Paul says, 'They will be judged on the basis of their conscience . . . which was bearing witness.' They had an awareness of right and wrong through the innate instinct of their conscience.

Just as the spirit of an artist lies within the pigments of his paintings, the spirit of your Maker lies within the wrinkles of your conscience. That doesn't negate the necessity of saving faith in Jesus but offers insight into how those who've never heard of Him will spend their eternity. In case you didn't know . . . eternal judgement is not our jurisdiction. The only one who votes and counts the votes is the sovereign God.

Live Like Him

So, you ask: If the best strategy for navigation in the spiritual realm is faith and awareness, what is the key for success? How do I use faith and awareness to win the battle? What is the strategy that implements those spiritual tools?

The answer is another crucial three words: *Live like Jesus.* It's just that simple and just that difficult. If you perfectly adopt his attitude and lifestyle, you'll have perfect peace. You obviously can't do that, but effort is everything with the Lord. Read and reside in the red letters and your life will never be in the red again. The word *truth* in the New Testament is usually synonymous with Jesus. Your life will battle the forces of Satan with the truth of Jesus. Guess who wins! There is one main theme of the New Testament—*live like Jesus.* The writers took the red letters and expanded them into letters that were read by early churches. Faith and awareness work beautifully when strategized by those three words.

My all-time favorite professor is Dr. Brandon Fredenburg of Lubbock Christian University. I studied under him at Lipscomb University. I am usually forced to read his writings twice to get my mind around them once, but they're always worth it. In the following quote, he reminds us that God makes living like Jesus easier with His mercy:

> Jesus begins his evangelizing with the word *repent.* Apparently, even John the Baptist missed it, as Matthew 11:1–15 makes clear. Jesus says those who even barely grasp his message have far greater insight than John. John's gospel of violent, fiery judgment, it seems,

put him at odds with Jesus's view of the nature of the kingdom of the heavens. "Repent," then, as Jesus uses it, retains its core meaning of "shift your paradigm" with reference to God and God's kingdom. For John, repentance focused on the personal sacrifices required for holiness; for Jesus, repentance kept its eyes on the merciful nature of God toward all persons (Exod. 34:5–7; Jonah 4:2b). "For I delight in mercy but not sacrifice; and in knowledge of God rather than burnt offerings" (Hos. 6:6, my translation).

Living like Jesus is not dependent on a 'personal sacrifice' checklist such as Sabbath rules, mandatory fasting, correct name on a church sign, acceptable words at baptism, appropriate Lord's Supper schedule, or other ecclesial things we've debated for two millennia. You choose your preference for those when you choose your church family. The key is faith in Jesus, not faith in church.

There are biblical examples of Christians practicing church expediencies in various ways. Some took the Lord's Supper every day (Acts 2), weekly (Acts 20), during Passover week (Ignatius), and whenever they chose (1 Corinthians 11). We have examples of them worshiping on Sunday, every day, Sabbath day, and anytime "two or three were gathered." Some sold all their belongings and shared them as one. Some early church worship included speaking in tongues and charismatic experiences of the Holy Spirit. The Corinthian churches added a spiritual love feast, and some met daily for both morning and evening worship. Jesus knew the church would take on different forms as it was ordained in different cultures. Today, the church form in Africa is very different from the form in Russia or Australia, but the function is the same—Live like Jesus.

The form of the large Jerusalem Church was different from the Corinthian house churches. The Jerusalem Church still practiced Jewish customs, while the Corinthian churches were influenced by the practices and mythology of the Greeks. Soon after Jesus's death, the Jerusalem church was worshiping in the temple daily. For the first couple AD centuries, some Christians continued to celebrate the Jewish feasts, seeing in them divine promises that were fulfilled in Christ. The seven churches of Asia, to which John wrote Revelation, were diverse and had bigger problems than debating which Bible version.

The one thing they all had in common was their desire to live like Jesus. That was the important thing! The New Testament is a story book, not a rule book. It's the story of Jesus, and we make every effort to rule our lives like His in order to find peace, salvation, and success.

Thus, true mental peace is found when the benchmarks of your physical body, social life, and full wallet are complemented by peace in the spiritual realm. You are primarily a spiritual being so primary peace is found when there is spiritual peace. Success in the spiritual realm predominates the other benchmarks. Michael W. Smith: "I've been there and done that—sold millions of records. That doesn't bring you peace." Happy people build their inner world; unhappy people blame their outer world. Living like Jesus brings peace.

Our Owner's Manual

You're thinking . . . *You* (me, that is) *have been quoting the Bible and basing your argument on that book.* How do you know it's credible? Where's the proof? No book has been so criticized, analyzed, or verified. Emperors have burned it, kings have cursed it, and dictators have banned it. But it's been translated into more than 3,000 languages and is still the best-selling book worldwide year after year. Over 100 million copies are sold annually with some 20 million copies sold in the U.S. alone.

It was written over the course of 1,500 years by forty different authors in thirteen different countries on three different continents without one single contradiction. Truly incredible! No other book can make that claim. A version of both testaments can be found in the Vatican library that dates back to the 300's AD. The Dead Sea Scrolls were found in the 1940s. They contained copies of Isaiah that date back to 900 BC and are identical to our copy today. God let them sit in that cave 3,000 years before bringing them out to strengthen our faith.

The Bible gives details with scientific accuracy that pre-date man's knowledge of the Earth being round. "God sits on the circle of the earth." (Isaiah 40). Job wrote 500 years before Christ, in a day when most people thought the earth was flat, that "God hangs the Earth on nothing." (Job 26) He also wrote about "rivers in the sea." (Job 38) Oceanographers didn't learn about those until centuries later.

The Old Testament has three hundred prophecies that predicted the coming of Jesus. Every single one was fulfilled with incredible accuracy. He would come through the lineage of David, be born of a virgin, called Immanuel, hang on a tree, go to Egypt, be a sinless suffering servant, teach in parables, start

His ministry in Galilee, have a forerunner like Elijah, enter Jerusalem on a donkey, be betrayed, have no bones broken but have hands and feet pierced, and be resurrected. Those details were all predicted hundreds of years before they were fulfilled. They are verified by both biblical and secular writings. Do you know of one single nonbiblical prophecy that was predicted with minute detail some five hundred years before it came true? And the Bible was written by approximately forty writers, most of whom had never met each other.

And yet, your decision to read and follow the Bible has an element of faith just like your interaction in the spiritual realm. That's just God being God. As those prophecies unfolded before the very eyes of Jews who studied their Bibles daily, most missed them. They knew the Scriptures but lacked faith and awareness.

Finding Success in the Realm

The purpose of this book is to offer insight for my grandchildren and all God's children that will lead them to a more successful, fulfilling life. So, what are detailed ways you can enhance your spiritual life to complement the other three benchmarks? How can you improve your faith and awareness? Increase your zeal for living like Jesus? Find inner peace in the spiritual realm? The following are ten tangible tips for better spiritual health.

1. The 20/20 hindsight eye chart contains the letters P-R-A-Y-E-R. The bifocal that brings faith and awareness into perfect focus is prayer. It's the anecdote for worry and the source for forgiveness. The only way to worry about nothing is to pray about everything. When life gets too hard to stand, learn to kneel. Real prayer is not just talking to God but listening to Him as well.

One of the great preachers of the Restoration Movement was Dr. Batsell Barrett Baxter. With a name like that, you'd have to be famous! He was a great preacher, teacher, and television personality with *The Herald of Truth*. He liked to talk about a night when he was a young boy. He walked by his dad's bedroom at dusk and saw the silhouette of him kneeling in prayer. That image was forever imprinted on Dr. Baxter's mind!

Faith/awareness are analogous to prayer/belief. "Whatever you ask for in prayer, believe you have received it and it will be yours." (Mark 11) Don't just pray for it but believe and expect it. You see the faith element again? It's always there. My special time to speak with the Lord is in bed. The direction of my tomorrow is determined by the discussions of my tonight.

2. The conversion experience is the small part. A preacher who preceded me at a church told me that the theme of every sermon he ever preached was salvation through baptism. I believe in baptism and believe it washes away our sins. I've been baptized in the Church of Christ, Baptist Church, and Jordan River!

But 99 percent of being a Christian is post-conversion and instructions, for the exact mode of conversion are not detailed in the New Testament. The thief on the cross was told he'd be in paradise after a mere confession while the Ethiopian eunuch was instructed by Phillip to be baptized on the basis of words from Isaiah. Some early converts received the Holy Spirit before baptism while others received the Spirit after baptism. John Calvin believed conversion to be an inner heart decision initiated by God. Billy Graham taught that conversion is an inner decision of the heart followed by believer's baptism. George Whitefield, the foremost Christian preacher of the eighteenth century, taught that conversion is a new birth—a change in the heart through the power of the Holy Spirit. The Amish descended from the Anabaptists (means baptized again— i.e., initially sprinkled but then immersed) and they place supreme emphasis on immersive baptism for salvation. The form of the church was probably mostly Catholic for more than one thousand years, and they believe conversion is "a movement away from sin, a re-ordering of priorities with Christ re-categorized as the center of our lives occurring through supernatural grace and the initiative of the Holy Spirit, first changing our hearts and minds, but then everyday actions." There are as many modes of conversion as there are denominations, but the most important part is deciding to live like Jesus. I've seen clear signs of Jesus working in the lives of people who experienced various modes of conversion.

The primary need for Christians in a church service is to be fed with spiritual manna for successful, godly living. We all struggle with sin and need encouragement. Jesus taught with parables, giving instructions for how to live a happy, peaceful life. In the beatitudes He listed ways lives are blessed in the kingdom. It was important to Him. The theme of the Sermon on the Mount is that right living leads to a right relationship with God which leads to a blessed life. Yes, I'm a Joel Osteen disciple.

When you get married, the wedding ceremony is important. The right documents must be signed, and the right words spoken, but 99 percent of a successful marriage depends on what happens after the ceremony. If a couple went for marriage counseling and were mostly instructed about the ceremony, it would be a waste of time. This illustration is not perfect because there are always people attending church services who need to hear about becoming a Christian, but the majority need encouragement for building more faith and awareness and learning to live like Jesus. "And we all, with unveiled faces, beholding the glory of the Lord, are being transformed into the same image from one degree of glory to another. For this comes from the Lord who is the Spirit." (2 Cor 3)

3. Daily Bible reading is life's best habit. When you fill your mind with God's words, there is less room for Satan's lies. The primary purpose for Bible reading is not to learn about the Bible but learn about God. I'm all for memorizing scriptures, but make sure you also "mimic-orize" them! The Bible is the only book for which you can believe everything you read! I've known people who didn't have a third-grade education but were a walking master's degree in Bible. They had more peace than most college professors.

My dad gave me a new NIV in 1983. If my house was on fire, it's the first thing I'd grab. I not only have notes from forty years of learning, but also a written record of reading the Bible entirely. I've been blessed to read it twenty-five times during the past forty years. I tell you that to motivate you to do better than me! My main Bible for reading now is *YouVersion* on my tablet, but I keep the reading record in my treasured NIV. I'm committed to reading it entirely each year I have left.

When you read, keep in mind that the theme of the entire Bible is living like Jesus. The narratives of the Old Testament have hidden undertones of the prophesied Jesus. The story of Jonah in the belly of a whale three days and nights only to come forth and preach to others is the subliminal story of Jesus. The letters of the New Testament are the story of the resurrected Jesus and ways the good news was spread around the world. After reading each paragraph, ask yourself, *What is the implication for living like Jesus?*

The Bible is written to be read in paragraphs, not 'plucked' or taught with proof text. A Jewish Rabbi named Nathan was the first to add verse numbers to the Old Testament in 1448, and Robert Estienne was the first to add verse numbers to the Vulgate translation of the New Testament in 1555. The scriptures were originally written on scrolls and read in paragraphs like a novel. Proof texting can be deceptive and not a true representation of the paragraph. Don't forget to read with the faith factor and listen to the Holy Spirit. Scripture is one of the main ways the triune God speaks to you and adds wellness to your spiritual health.

4. Worship is a spiritual transfusion. Just as a blood transfusion gives life to your body, worship gives life to your soul. I believe worship is the primary blessing of corporate gatherings. I've visited churches that allotted 10-12 minutes for worship/prayer and 45 minutes for preaching. I prefer 50/50. The Spirit speaks to my heart in worship and enriches my status in the spiritual realm. The word *worship* comes from the word *worthiness*. God is worthy of worship because he loves you more than anyone and reciprocates with blessings. You're created in His image and become most like that image through worship.

Worship is a celebration. I've never understood how Christians can attend a ballgame to celebrate but attend a church service to meditate. I've been to some funerals that celebrated more than some worship services! I'm all for reverence, but King David's worship was a celebration. He often used the word *rejoice* to describe his worship. Same for the apostle Paul, who used that word as a verb and command. It's hard to rejoice without celebrating. If someone gave you $100 million, you'd be beyond thankful and want to celebrate! Worship is your celebratory response to the Lord for giving the gift of salvation.

Andrew Greer is one of America's foremost worship leaders. He writes about spending an entire week in complete silence with the monks at Abbey of our Lady in Gethsemani, in New Haven, Kentucky. "Tonight, I joined the monks in their daily compline—prayers for the end of the day. As I knelt, and they sang, it all blended together. My posture down low, their prayers lifted high. It felt like some kind of Bob Ross watercolor. Or a Mister Rogers song. Like my mom's hug. Or my dad's, "Love you, son." Real worship is transforming.

Worship is daily and personal, not just a Sunday morning checkmark. It's an endless soul satisfier. It's not a part of your life; it *is* your life. Meditation and reverence are perfect for private reflection. Every time I experience a bit of good news, I silently rejoice and praise the Lord. I narrowly avoided a bad car accident recently, so I pulled my car to the side of the road and worshipped the Lord. Your public worship is richer on the first day of the week when your private worship is richer every day of the week.

5. Blameless living brings true peace. *If you can remember only one sentence from this book, memorize that one.* I have tested the Lord with this principle for fifty years. I have read its truth over and over in both the Old and New Testaments. I've seen it played out in the lives of others. Blameless living will protect you from what you thought you wanted and bless you with what you didn't think you needed. The sun is always shining brightly in a spotless mind. Being blameless is the best good luck.

Airplanes can fly on auto pilot without human assistance through software programs that utilize hydraulic, mechanical, and electronic systems to control the plane. It's like car cruise control. I've learned that when my life is blameless, the Lord controls the outcome with auto pilot. I don't have to worry about how things will work out. All fear is gone. The Lord has me in the palm of His hand. "Mark the blameless man and observe the upright; for the future of that man is peace." (Psalm 37)

What is blameless living? It's when your thoughts, actions, and intentions are living like Jesus. You say, "You're taking all the fun out of my life!" I say, "You try living it just one month and see how much peace (and fun) you have!" Try it for one month and see how much better your body feels. How much better your blood flows. How much better you sleep. How much better your relationships flow. Blameless does not mean perfect but living innocently of intentional wrongdoing and without guilt.

David wrote, "Lord, who may dwell in your sacred tent? Who may live on your holy mountain? The one whose walk is *blameless*, who does what is righteous, who speaks the truth from the heart; whose tongue utters no slander, who does no wrong to a neighbor and casts no slur on others." (Psalm 15) There is no pillow so soft as a clear conscience.

Men struggle with lust, women with gossip. We all struggle with hatred, unforgiveness, spite, and bitterness. We watch and read things that poison our minds. We surf the Internet for visual trash. We're selfish, greedy, fleshly, hypocritical, jealous, and deceitful. We're impatient in traffic and at the grocery store. We wallow in others' defeats. Our worship is hollow. We don't read God's Word every day. Those are all things we can correct. I drive through cities and see people standing on street corners who are obviously frustrated, angry, poor, and without hope. I think to myself, *If they only knew!* Give God your weakness and he'll give you His strength.

When my life is not going well, it always dawns on me to check my blameless meter. When I worry about my finances, when my relationship with my wife and other family is a struggle, when my blood pressure is elevated, when my worship is hindered, and when I'm just generally not content, I analyze my meter and remember my life is not blameless.

But conversely, when my thoughts, actions, and intentions are pure and focused on walking closely with the Lord, my life is happy, peaceful, and healthy. Success is everywhere; worry is gone. All things are working together for good. Those are the times when I can see the Lord has me on auto pilot. I don't have to worry about how it turns out because it's not my problem. I've read the last chapter and know how it ends.

What's the toughest time to be blameless? When I'm on top of the world! When my finances are great, and I don't think I need any help. When I have friends to spare and feel extra healthy. But I have learned to beware of those times. Satan uses them to trap me and encourage me to live idolatrously, worshiping things rather than the Maker.

6. You can't out-give God. I wish I had learned this principle earlier in life. I'm the world's best justifier! For many years I didn't tithe, justifying that I was rearing Christian children, paying for Christian education, and serving as a Christian pastor. But when I began the discipline of regular tithing, my bank account began regular growing. There is no other explanation! Like a golf grip that felt wrong at first, the tithing cloud lifted. I now relish giving and know my sacrifice will be returned twice . . . or thrice.

I've observed that successful people enjoy giving. It *is* more blessed to give than receive. Someone said money might not buy happiness but giving it away will. Warren Buffett has a net worth of $100 billion and has pledged to give away 99 percent. I was present when the Ezell Center was dedicated at Lipscomb University. The Ezells became wealthy through Purity Dairies and donated $13 million to the construction of that building. It was one of their best days.

John D. Rockefeller was the wealthiest man in America in the early twentieth century. He donated $500 million to charitable causes and his initiatives continue to this day. Bill Gates recently bequeathed $20 billion and intends to donate his entire $113 billion fortune. Andrew Carnegie gave away 90 percent of his wealth in his last eighteen years. Only by giving do we receive more than we possess. Giving to others is the greatest gift you can give yourself. You will retain what you will bestow.

You ask—how much should a Christian give? In the Old Testament, the tithe is usually regarded as 10 percent, but the principle of giving in the New Testament is the same as the Old Testament. The key word is not *tithe* but *sacrifice*. In the OT, God commanded the Jews to give the unblemished lamb from their herd, their best. If it didn't hurt a little, it wasn't a sacrifice. "Honor the Lord with your wealth and the first fruits of your produce." (Prov 3) The same is true for Christians today. To find true success and peace in the spiritual realm, make a weekly financial sacrifice to the One who's fighting your spiritual battles.

If your income is $1,500 a week, a $20 offering is not much of a sacrifice. I remember Dad saying, "If your weekly offering is less than your Sunday lunch at the local restaurant, it might not be enough!" My friend, Carlos Jacobs said that anytime he and Jeanette were running low on money, they would increase their offering. Worked every time! We all know the point when a gift becomes a sacrifice on the offering meter.

We are inundated with charitable organizations wanting our money— United Way, World Vision, Red Cross, St. Jude's, and others. They all do good work and I've made donations, but if you want the Lord to bless your life, your first obligation is to Him on Sunday morning! "No man should appear before the Lord empty-handed. Each of you must bring a gift in proportion to the way the Lord has blessed you." (Deuteronomy 16)

Jesus said more about giving than any other subject because money is very dear to our hearts. Without it, we're helpless. His words, "Give, and it will be given to you. A good measure, pressed down, shaken together, and running over, will be poured into your lap. For with the measure you use, it will be measured to you." (Luke 6) And when God blesses you financially, don't just raise your standard of living but raise your standard of giving. Billy Graham, "God has given us two hands. One to receive with and the other to give with."

One of my favorite statements in the Bible is in Malachi 3, "Bring the whole tithe into the storehouse, that there may be food in my house. *Test* me in this," says the LORD Almighty, "and see if I will not throw open the flood-gates of heaven and pour out so much blessing that there will not be room enough to store it." The secret of success is in the test. Generous giving results in bigger living.

The main theme of the Old Testament is that God is a jealous God who wants your undivided attention. Yes, he wants you to have lots of money and a great life, but only when you give Him the credit and your full attention! There is not one dime in your bank account that didn't come from Him. He created it all and owns it all. You're just a caretaker for your time on Earth. "Remember the Lord your God who gives you the ability to produce wealth." (Deuteronomy 8)

7. A trip to the Holy Land seals the deal. I'm known preachers who be-lieved the King James Version was dropped out of a Heavenly helicopter, the 'denominations' should switch the "n" and "m" because they're filled with demons, and that Acts 2:38 is the only verse in the Bible that really matters. Most of them were taught by other sincere men who had a bad education and never traveled abroad.

A trip to the Holy Land will do two things—broaden your concept of the word *Christian* and increase your faith in the Bible. There are people living there who love Jesus and walk with Him every day who've never heard of Baptist, Methodist, Presbyterian, or Church of Christ. They've been members of the Greek Orthodox, Armenian Apostolic, or other Christian church all their life. Their Bible is not the King James Version because theirs is not translated into English but into their native tongue of Modern Hebrew or Arabic. The King James dialect does not work when translated into other languages. They've never been taught that it's scriptural to have three songs, a prayer, and one more song before the sermon. Their worship would be a different experience, one that embraces their culture and upbringing.

I remember visiting the Spring of Harod, where Gideon took his men to drink. Some lapped like a dog as others cupped their hands. (Judges 6-8) That incident happened three thousand years ago, but the Spring is still there today! And I'll never forget standing in downtown Jericho. I looked to the west and saw the wilderness of Judea where Jesus was tempted; to the east the Jordan River through which the Israelites came into the promised land; to the south is the Dead Sea; and to the north the ruins of the walls of Jericho. It's all still there just like the Bible describes it! Very faith-building!!

You can see the ancient walls of the temple that Solomon built along with the temple walls Herod rebuilt. I remember walking in the valley of Elah where David killed Goliath; seeing the eleven caves near Qumran where the Dead Sea Scrolls were found; riding in a boat on the Sea of Galilee where Jesus walked on the water; and visiting a house in Capernaum which has the inscription 'Petros' on a stone. Peter mentions his mother-in-law's house in Capernaum in his teachings and might have lived there!

Yes, the Lord created you to be a creature of faith but the closest you'll come to proof is a trip to the Holy Land. The fact that Israel is a small country surrounded by its enemies but protected by the Lord is also a faith builder. You invest in a house, lawn, automobile, and sports team, why not invest in your faith and visit the Holy Land? It's a shortcut to spiritual health.

8. Church history gives clarity. Beliefs seek as many facts as possible. Modern communication makes it possible for people in Memphis, Tennessee, in 2023 AD to have the facts about what happened in Memphis, Egypt, in 3023 BC. The Lord has preserved clear records of the history of mankind for those five thousand years. We have facts about how the New Testament books were compiled as the Muratorian Canon in the second century. We have facts about the Bible's translation into Latin by Jerome in the late 300s to John Wycliffe's translation into English in the late 1300s to Luther's translation into German in the 1500s. The facts of the past cannot be changed by the opinions of the present.

We have writings about church history from Justin Martyr (AD 150), Tertullian (AD 200), and Cyprian (AD 250). Eusebius wrote a chronological history of the church that covered the first through fourth centuries. We have the 5th century writings of Augustine and Chrysostom. Anselm, Aquinas, and a' Kempis give factual insight into the church of the Middle Ages (6th – 16th centuries). Luther, Calvin, Knox, and others wrote volumes during the Reformation (17th century). Just as we have historical facts about the Roman Empire, we have historical facts about the church spreading from Jerusalem to Judea and to all the world—from Pentecost to Catholicism to Protestantism and other groups along the way.

I visited the Louvre Museum in Paris. As a visitor walks through the huge rooms filled with famous paintings, the main theme seems to be Jesus Christ. There are paintings of the cross, Mary Magdalene, and the head of John the Baptist on a platter. Artists have depicted the miracles of Jesus and His resurrection. Many of the paintings date back to the Middle Ages (AD 400-1400). I observed the same in Buckingham Palace in London. It's clear Jesus has been on the minds of the people of the Earth throughout the centuries.

Part of my life's history was being reared in a church that considered it a sin to worship with an instrument. Those holding that belief were some of the finest Christians on this earth who were a product of their religious upbringing, but secular and theological history are two of the best ways to get clarity for that tradition.

It's clear from biblical history that instrumental worship was a part of temple worship. And the apostle Paul planted several New Testament churches in synagogues that were 'mini temples' which gave Jews who didn't live close to the temple a place to worship.

According to church history, the song book of the early church was Psalms and instrumental worship is suggested for many of them. "To be accompanied by stringed instruments" is in the prelude for Psalm 54, 55, 61, 67, 76, and 81. The root word for *psalm* is *psallein* which means "a song or hymn sung with a stringed instrument." The apostle Paul prescribed that Psalms be used in Christian worship (Ephesians 5).

The Psalms not only suggest that instruments of worship accompany singing, but they were also used as actual instruments to praise God. "Praise him with a blast of the ram's horn; praise him with the lyre and harp! Praise him with the tambourine and dancing; praise him with strings and flutes! Praise him with a clash of cymbals; praise him with loud clanging cymbals." (Psalms 150:3-5. And the book of Revelation reveals that the angels are worshipping the Lord with an instrument in Heaven.

Secular church history tells us that the noninstrumental tradition grew mostly out of Civil War animosity between Restoration Movement Christians that were north and south of the Mason Dixon line. Their fierce debates led to a split between the Independent Christian Church denomination (north) and the Church of Christ denomination (south), officially in 1906. This eventually led to acapella worship being taken to the extreme of being a salvation issue (sin). Dr. Douglas A. Foster has written some excellent books on church history including *The Stone-Campbell Movement—A Global History*.

Both biblical and church history give insight into the discussion of form versus function. Is the form of church (way it's implemented) more important? Or is the function of church (living like Jesus) more important? I believe the New Testament's style and general content indicates function predominates form. We cannot solve all the form questions, but the function is agreed by all—live like Jesus in order to live with Jesus. Faith makes more sense when history gives pretense. Small facts lead to much clarity. The great Bill Gaither: "The church at its worst is better than the world at its best."

9. Discovering life's purpose is God's plan. Living with a sense of purpose brings success. We all want direction and meaning for each day. Most people live aimlessly, just bouncing from crisis to crisis. What is your purpose in life? What do you live to accomplish? "Before I shaped you in the womb, I knew all about you. Before you saw the light of day, I had plans for you." (Jeremiah 1)

One Saturday night a few years ago I had the thrill of worshipping with Rick Warren at Saddleback Church in Los Angeles. He has written extensively about finding our purpose. "Do you want to live a life of purpose and meaning? Think of what you do well—and find ways to do more of those things. Then think of what you *don't* do well—and find ways to do less of those things. No matter what, you can rest in the truth that God is working in your life and shaped you to succeed." Rick believes if you find your passion, you'll find your purpose.

King David was a warrior. He wanted his life's purpose to be building the temple, but that was not God's plan. David's life purpose was to build a dynasty and create a lineage through which the Messiah would come. Solomon's life purpose was to build the temple.

The apostle Paul thought his purpose was to persecute Christians, but learned it was to convert new Christians. Matthew believed his purpose was to be a tax collector, but realized it was to be an apostle. Peter assumed his purpose was to be a fisherman, but found it was to be a fisher of men. When you discover your purpose, you'll uncover a vital aspect of the secret.

I believe one of my purposes is to be an encourager. I hope you sense that in this book. I wish my name was Barnabas—a son of encouragement. I enjoy encouraging young pastors, children, grandchildren, and others who need a good word. Sometimes the gift of a genuine word of encouragement is more valuable than a gift of $10,000. My most recent calling is 'grandfather'. . . a life purpose like no other!

I remember as a young teenager making one of my first public speeches. I was sooo nervous. I felt like the crowd could only sense my nervousness. When I got home after the speech, the phone was ringing. It was a sweet lady, "That was one of the best speeches I've ever heard. I could have listened to you for hours." I was too young to realize she was being prescriptive rather than descriptive, but it was worth more than many dollars to me.

Mark Twain: "The two most important days in your life are the day you were born and the day you figure out why." Your purpose in life is not what you do for a living, it's what you live to do. I know people whose purpose is deer hunting, Tennessee Titans, Planet Fitness, or Little League baseball. Just as you get acquainted with your next-door neighbor, get acquainted with yourself and discover your God-given purpose. It will provide meaning for your life which will complement every aspect of true success.

10. A life of faith makes dying easier. Death is the ultimate curse for Adam's sin. Death has not been easy for one single person but eventually comes to every single person. Having served as a pastor, I've stood at the bedside of dying people. No matter how saintly their life, the uncertainty of death is a frightening moment. There is only one way to soften the blow—deep faith in the promise of being in a better place. Writers in the first century said of Christians, "They die differently."

Christian recording artist Rory Feek lost his beautiful wife, Joey, to cancer. They both faced it with brave and beautiful faith. He writes, "Even the bad stuff, in a strange way, was actually the good stuff. It's what got me to where I am, and made me who I am, and it will be a part of leading me to where I need to be."

I remember the day Dad died. He was in Cleveland Clinic (OH) awaiting a heart transplant. We didn't expect him to die so quickly, but Mom called and said his kidneys were shutting down. So, we children flew back to Cleveland and gathered around his bed. We told him we loved him, and it was clear, even in his semi-conscious state, that it brought him peace. It was like he waited to die until we got there to tell him good-bye. It's no fun to die alone and without faith.

The most memorable death of my childhood was Ken McDonald. He was an eighth grader when I was a seventh grader. We were good friends. His Mom found him dead in his sleep one Saturday morning during that school year. No foul play, just a freak heart attack. Death is a tougher experience for younger survivors. To see Ken in that casket and realize his soul was in eternity was a life-changing experience. A life of deep faith makes dying easier for the dead and the living. Faith is the balm that soothes the soul on the deathbed.

Success Is a Whole Number

One of my favorite high school teachers was Mrs. Carothers. She taught biology which became my college major. I remember a student asking her one day, "Do you believe plants communicate with each other like animals?" Her answer was, "No, because they don't have a central nervous system like animals." I have reflected on that through the years. No, they don't communicate with each other, but they do communicate with their Creator. A cluster of daffodils all face the same direction when they bloom, toward the sun. All plant life is responsive to the One who made them. And so, your personal spiritual realm does not communicate with your friend's realm but with the heavenly realm of the Holy Spirit. We all bloom brighter when we face the Son. I hope you have a clearer insight into that spiritual existence after reading this chapter. Mother Teresa got this one right!

And the Winner Is . . .

I asked these questions in the first paragraph of the book—How would you define success? What's the secret? Is it mostly financial? Mostly mental? When you see the word success, who comes to mind? Who was the most successful person of your childhood? Why?

It took 44,349 words, 2,555 paragraphs, and 6,128 lines to answer those questions. The definition of true success is marked by four benchmarks: physical well-being, social vitality, abundant wealth, and spiritual health. If those serve as your life's barometer, your atmospheric pressure meter will point to peace. It's not enough to win the war of life in just a few areas because success results from signing a peace treaty with your whole person.

And if the personal examples listed in chapter 1 are a multiple-choice quiz, the correct answer is B) President Carter. Good health at ninety-seven years, marvelous social skills, abundant wealth, and peace in the spiritual realm have characterized his life. And yes, I'm a lifelong Republican!

EPILOGUE:
Benchmarkers

S UCCESS BREEDS SUCCESS. Learning comes from two teachers—personal experience and others' experience. The latter can be a shortcut because the school of life is always open. Our candles are lit by the flame of example. This final chapter is an opportunity to learn from some people whose 'life bench' is notched by all four marks. High tide floats all ships.

One of the special blessings of ministry is crossing paths with great lives. Two of those were Dr. Russ & Rosemary Burcham. Russ was a dentist in Kennett, Missouri. I remember him telling me that when fluoride was added to drinking water in the 1950s, he saw an 80 percent reduction of cavities. I have never forgotten that statistic. The Burchams were model benchmarks. She hosted a fifteen-minute human interest TV program each weeknight, the subject of which was the interesting folks of the Missouri Bootheel. It seemed like every boot in heel watched that program. Her motivation was to keep them on the channel so they would watch the fifteen-minute Bible teaching program that followed. It was hosted by the Slicer Street Church preacher (yours truly). It was a brilliant win-win. When the Burchams retired, they spent several months each year doing foreign mission work—one working on teeth, the other working on souls. They were healthy, wealthy, and friendly, but their life was mostly about being steadfast, immovable, and always abounding in good works.

My all-time favorite athlete is Mike Rhodes. He was reared in Perry County shooting a muddy basketball to a makeshift goal on the side of a barn. Those sloppy practices resulted in Perry County winning back-to-back high school state championships. He averaged forty-one points per game and was the state's leading scorer in his senior year. He signed with Vanderbilt and broke Clyde Lee's freshman scoring record. He was named SEC Freshman of the Year. His career was marred by a coaching change. His beloved initial coach, Wayne Dobbs, was dismissed by the university. The school chose between hiring Richard Schmidt or Mike Krzyzewski as a replacement. They chose Schmidt and the rest is history. Schmidt wanted to play his new recruits and minimize the SEC's best player, but Mike's secret is his great attitude. He kept his head up, still led the team in scoring, and was named First Team All-SEC. Although his senior season did not go exactly as hoped due to injury and Schmidt, he still graduated as the school's all-time leading scorer. The key to Mike's positive attitude is his faith in Jesus. He's been an elder of a church for many years and is a model husband, father, grandfather, and citizen. He is also a successful engineer. Mike Rhodes is the epitome of the four benchmarks of success.

Don Lowe was a self-made millionaire in a small town. Demopolis, Alabama, is not exactly the place most people would choose to make their fortune with a jewelry store. But Don was blessed with a winning personality and an eight-days-a-week work ethic. As he made money, he re-invested it in rental property and made more money. He was my dad's brother-in-law and like Warren Buffett, enjoyed being generous. When Dad was a teenager, he'd spend the night with Don & Jeanette. When he woke up each morning, a $20 bill would have miraculously appeared in his pants pocket. Don served on the board at Faulkner University where he was also a great benefactor. He has been with the Lord twenty-five years now, but Uncle Don will always be remembered as a successful, honest, and kind Christian who loved to bless other lives. The best exercise for the heart is generosity.

When we moved to Blanchester, Ohio, I was told to make sure I visited Shirley Vallee. She was the wealthiest person in town, very generous, and a member of our church. I went straight to her house . . . and learned she was also a dedicated Christian. She was the widow of Richard Vallee, who had been a successful chemist. He was also a stock market guru and owned a nursing home. He handled the finances and Shirley knew they were in good shape, but apparently didn't realize the full extent. They lived in a very modest house in a middle-class neighborhood. After his death she learned she was worth $13 million! She proceeded to give it away! She gave hundreds of thousands to our church. She paid for a new kitchen, new paved parking lot, and untold thousands with her offering. She also gave more than $100,000 to the local senior citizens center and who knows how much to people all over town. She received a wonderful legacy and left one behind.

How could I write a book about success without including the name Dolly Parton. She grew up in a one-bedroom cabin near Sevierville as the fourth of twelve children. Her dad was a poor tobacco farmer and construction worker who couldn't read or write. He paid the doctor a sack of oatmeal to deliver Dolly at birth. Bill Owens arranged for her to appear on Cas Walker's WVIK radio program at age ten and the rest is history. She's a true American hero who is a benchmark among benchmarks. She follows a low-carb diet, has been married to her first husband fifty-six years, has a net worth of $600 million, and is a dedicated Christian. Her grandfather was a Pentecostal preacher. She gave millions to residents of Gatlinburg after the fire, gave millions to fight Covid, and gives millions each year to her Imagination Library. She also owns three hundred wigs and plays six musical instruments--dulcimer, banjo, guitar, piano, recorder, and saxophone. One of her best quotes: "We cannot direct the wind, but we can adjust the sails."

One of the most successful men of my childhood was Coach John Wooden. Born in Hall, Indiana, in 1910, he led Martinsville High to a state championship in 1927. He was named All-State three times. He attended Purdue University and was the first guard to be named All-American three times. He was chosen to coach UCLA basketball in 1948 with a salary of $6,000 per year. He would win ten NCAA national championships with the Bruins. He was not only a great coach, but also a great husband. He was married to Nellie Riley fifty-three years until her death on March 21, 1985. After she passed, he visited her grave on the twenty-first day of every month and wrote her a letter (I believe each time!) saying how much he missed her and couldn't wait to see her again. He then folded it once, slid it into a little envelope, and put it on the stack of love letters he kept on her bed pillow. The stack had more than 180 letters. In her memory, he slept only on his half of the bed, only on his pillow, only on top of the sheets, never between them, and with just the old bedspread they shared covering him. He was not comfortable between the sheets without her. He was a devout Christian who read his Bible daily and regarded 1 Corinthians 13 his favorite chapter. He died just four months shy of age one hundred. They don't make many like the 'Wizard of West-wood.'

Pat Boone has sold fifty million records and is sixteenth on the list of all-time records ever sold. From PatBoone.com, he's not just a singer but an actor, TV host, producer, songwriter, author, motivational speaker, TV pitch-man, radio personality, record company head, TV station owner, sports team owner, family man, and humanitarian. At age eighty-eight he's still very active as national spokesman for the 60 Plus Association. They hear him on two nationally syndicated radio shows—*The Music of Your Life* and *The Pat Boone Show*, which features contemporary gospel music. Pat and Shirley (Foley) Boone (daughter of Country star 'Red' Foley) were married for more than sixty-five years before her death. "We lived a wonderful, blessed life together. I've parted with my better half for a little while . . . but we don't die, we just move on to another place, and today (January 11, 2019) was moving day," Pat said of his high school sweetheart. "She's changed her address, that's all, and moved to a different mansion that I expect to join her in one day." My dad attended Lipscomb University with Pat in the 1950s. His net worth is estimated at $50 million. The good Lord has kept Pat Boone on this earth a long time for a lot of good reasons.

A more contemporary success story is Carrie Underwood. She was born in 1983 and grew up on a farm in rural Oklahoma. Like many country stars, she grew up singing in church. She attended Northeast State University where she graduated magna cum laude. She entered the *American Idol* contest in 2004 because it helped her get school credit toward her degree in mass communication. When she won the contest in 2005, it kickstarted her country music career. Today she's married to hockey star Mike Fisher, and they have a net worth of $140 million. They are raising a fine family and attend GracePointe Church in Nashville. She says, "I'm a suck-it-up-and-move-on kind of person. Every day is a new day, and you'll never find happiness unless you move on."

My favorite President was Ronald Reagan. Janet and I married in 1979. The economy and nation were in the ditch. Reagan pulled us out. He grew up in Dixon, Illinois, the son of a shoe salesman. As a child, he attended the Disciples of Christ Church and graduated Dixon High as a star athlete and student body president. He worked as a lifeguard in the summer and reportedly saved seventy-seven lives. He attended Eureka College, where he played football, ran track, captained the swim team, served as student body president, and starred in school plays. His first job was as a radio sports announcer. While in southern California covering the Chicago Cubs for spring training, he auditioned at Warner Brothers. They signed him to a contract, and he debuted in *Love Is in the Air* in 1937. Over the next three decades he starred in fifty films. His first political experience was being elected president of the Screen Actors Guild. Starting out as a Democrat but changing to a Republican, he was elected governor of California and a two-term U.S. president. I like his quote: "Live simply, love generously, care deeply, speak kindly, leave the rest to God." One of the highlights of my life was visiting his grave in Simi Valley, California. It was an emotional experience, paying respects to a man who had done so much for my life. Inscribed on his tombstone are the words, "I know in my heart that man is good, that what is right will eventually triumph, and there is purpose and worth to each and every life."

Reg Gipson was valedictorian of my high school class. To my knowledge, he is the first African American to achieve that honor at my alma mater. Nobody saw color in Reg, and he treated everybody the same. I remember the first time I saw him. I was on the Hickman County Junior High basketball team, and he was on the East Hickman Junior High basketball team. When the game was over, I'd seen way too much of him! It was a massacre, and I was on the massacred end. He was not only a star in the classroom but also on the court. The East students came to Hickman County High after eighth grade, so thankfully he was on my team in high school. He graduated from the University of Tennessee with a degree in mechanical engineering and was a successful manager at Proctor & Gamble for thirty-two years. They sent him all over the world, including a stint in Malaysia. He and his wife, Nancy, are model benchmarks who've been together since high school. High on the list of Hickman County's finest ever is Reginald Gipson. And the student who asked Mrs. Caruthers that question? You guessed it!

Tim Tebow is a perfect role model for any young person. He was born to Baptist missionaries in the Philippines and returned to live in Jacksonville, Florida, when he was three years old. He was homeschooled, but Florida allows those students to compete in high school sports. He led Nease High to the 4A state title, attended Florida University, and led them to two SEC titles, two NCAA titles, and won the Heisman. He signed with the Denver Broncos and was criticized for "Tebowing" or kneeling on one knee in prayer after a touchdown. He established the Tim Tebow Foundation in 2010 through which he provides food, clothing, housing, medication, and the good news of the gospel to orphans in seven countries. He opened CURE hospital in Davao City, Philippines, in 2014. His other charities include Uncle Dick's Orphanage and Shands Hospital. He has written two books—*Shaken* and *This Is the Day* both of which are *New York Times* bestsellers. He married South African model and former Miss Universe Demi-Leigh Nel-Peters in 2020. He was a self-proclaimed virgin until marriage. When they were wed, he had a net worth of $10 million and she $5 million. If you're looking a high-profile athlete who uses his fame to glorify God, it's Tim Tebow!

Joyce Meyer is one America's most sought-after speakers. Her distinguished life has been characterized by overcoming obstacles. She was abused sexually and emotionally by her father, a World War II survivor. She married a part-time car salesman, but they soon divorced. She then met Dave Meyer and credits him with turning her life around. They've been married fifty-three years. While praying in 1976, she believes God verbally called her name and she began airing fifteen-minute radio broadcasts called "Life in the Word." Writing and speaking soon followed. She's written a hundred books and speaks to hundreds of thousands of people each year. More recently she was diagnosed with breast cancer but overcame another obstacle. She has a net worth of $8 million and has been criticized for her extravagant lifestyle, but she says the Lord has blessed her and wants her to enjoy. I totally agree, Joyce. She's taken a bad life and turned it into a great life. Victory is sweetest when you've known defeat.

Cornelius Vanderbilt rose from absolutely zilch to become the wealthiest American of the nineteenth century. His parents were poor farmers on famed Staten Island, but his father made a little extra money ferrying fresh produce to Manhattan. Cornelius was intrigued by boating and started studying shipbuilding. He acquired a small fleet while in his late twenties. He married his first cousin, Sophia Johnson, and they had thirteen children. In the 1820s, Cornelius started building steamships and operating a prosperous ferry. He was known for his ruthless business tactics, driving the weak competition out of business. During California's legendary gold rush, he developed a steamship service that transported people from New York to San Francisco via a route across Nicaragua. He was earning more than $1 million a year ($26 million in today's money). Others were following a longer path around the tip of South America. He would also make money with the railroad in the 1860s and was the driving force behind the construction of Manhattan's Grand

Depot. He died in 1877 with a fortune of $100 million and left most of it to his son, William. He was not known for extreme philanthropy like the Carnegies or Rockefellers, but he did give $1 million to build and endow Vanderbilt University in 1873. I'm not certain he checked off all four benchmarks for success, but since I'm a lifelong Vandy fan, he gets a pass!

I'm writing the following paragraphs early on a Sunday morning, remembering one of the finest Sunday morning Christians my life intersected. Carlos Jacobs was a leader of the church and a great mentor to a young man in his late twenties. One day we were riding in his old Ford truck when he asked, "May I share my life story with you?" I had no idea!

His parents abandoned him when he was three years old. He could still see the graphic details in his mind's eye. They locked him and his older sister in a tool shack on the failing family farm. "As they closed the door, I saw tears in Mom's eyes and knew something was wrong," he said. In about an hour, the Macon County sheriff unlocked the door and rescued them. They were placed in separate foster homes. The older sister never really recovered.

"I grew-up with a burning desire to kill my dad," Carlos said. "Thought about it every day!" He finished high school and joined the army to vent his anger. After serving his country, he began a search for his parents' whereabouts, starting with his dad, and learned he was living in Indianapolis. He bought a big Bowie knife that he could conceal in an Army boot and got a bus ticket to Indy. When he arrived, he took a taxi to the address. It took him to the rough side of town and as the cabby turned onto his dad's street, he noticed a rough-looking man staggering down the sidewalk. It was mid-morning, and the man was drunk. That was his dad.

"Stop right here!" he said to the driver as he stepped out of the cab and walked over to the man. "Hi, Dad, I'm Carlos. The son you abandoned!" he shouted as he grabbed his father's soiled shirt collar. His dad teared up, asking with a sheepish stutter, "Why have you come back?" Carlos replied with rage, "To kill you . . . you worthless 'so-and-so,' but where's my mama?" His dad pointed down the street.

Carlos walked down the sidewalk to a dilapidated shack with a resemblance to the one in Macon County. He knocked on the half-hinged door. His mom hadn't seen him in twenty-five years, but immediately recognized the face of her only son. "Oh, Carlos, why have you come back?" she asked with tears forming. "To kill Dad!! That's why!!" as he showed her the knife. She said, "Oh son, please don't ruin your life because of him. He's been nothing but a worthless, lazy drunk all these years. You have a long life ahead of you. Please, please." Carlos talked to her for a few more minutes, shared her tears, and then an embrace. He boarded the Greyhound bus back to Nashville, still filled with rage.

After his return home, he met Jeanette Creason. She was not only a beautiful young lady, but a beautiful young Christian lady. They fell in love and Carlos started going to church. They got married and he became active in the church. He was appointed to the office of deacon and started teaching Sunday School class. He was reading his Bible every day and learning from the teachings of Dr. Marlin Connelly. He and Jeanette became parents of a precious little girl. When the Lord starts working on a life, the old person is often hardly recognizable.

A few more years passed, and Carlos continued to grow "in wisdom and stature and in favor with God and man." And one day he decided to get back on that Greyhound to Indy, hail another yellow taxi to his parents' house, and knock on that half-hinged door. His mom answered through the torn screen, "Oh, Carlos, why have you come back?" He said, "Mom, you and dad are obviously in bad health and struggling financially. I have a nice basement apartment at my house and a good job with Sealtest. Would you come live with me? I want to take care of you both for the rest of your days." To forgive is to set a prisoner free and realize the prisoner is you.

Carlos Jacobs's changed life was a considerable influence on changing my life in my earlier years. He has been with the Lord many years now, but I look forward to hearing his story again and meeting his parents one day. He was successful financially, physically, socially, and can check off all the marks. Is there somebody in your life that needs forgiveness... for your sake?

Post It

Success is the ambition of every human. The secret of success is the discovery of just a few. The result of discovering the secret is a life of true peace and happiness. To be happy with your *health* and weight brings gratification. To be at peace with others brings *social* satisfaction. To be *financially* independent brings confidence. And to be victorious in *spiritual* battles brings supernatural blessing. But to live a life with all four attributes complementing each other is the ultimate secret of success.

Achieving the benchmarks is not just the whim of the few, but the potential of every single person. *Every* single reader! Yes, the road to success is dotted with many tempting parking spaces, but the journey is only complete when it never ends. As we begin, we must realize the stairs work better than the elevator, taking just one at a time. But as we taste small daily victories, the palate of life begins to savor and suppose each satisfying morsel of success.

Write "benchmark" on a slice of Post-It note and stick it to the top of your laptop. Remind yourself every day of four words: *physical, social, financial, spiritual* . . . and enjoy the success. Life is too short to live without it.

Thanks for taking this journey with me. I've been mentally processing this book for fifteen years, proving its truth through my life experiences. It is my prayer that my grandchildren (and all God's children) will live a richer, more peaceful life because it is characterized by the benchmarks of success.

THE AUTHOR

A UTHOR LARRY ROGERS MENTALLY PROCESSED THIS BOOK FOR FIFTEEN YEARS, proving it through his life's experiences. He grew up in a small town but spent most of his life in a big city. He has served as an ordained pastor for three denominations, worked as a licensed health insurance agent, and owned a landscape design business. He is also a master gardener, Mediterranean diet chef, avid world traveler, author of two previous books, and daily stock market trader. He has two master's degrees (Lipscomb University, Harding School of Theology) and studied at Beeson Divinity School Doctor of Ministry program. He is a parent and a grandparent. He has never stopped learning because life has never stopped teaching. This book will help you discover the true secret of success.

Made in the USA
Columbia, SC
27 October 2023